English Language Learners

ABOUT THE NATIONAL ASSOCIATION FOR MULTICULTURAL EDUCATION (NAME) SERIES

Editors: Abul Pitre and Ashraf Esmail

Educators in the twenty-first century face enormous challenges as a result of No Child Left Behind and Race to the Top. The requirements embedded into these high-accountability policies have exacerbated the disparities that exist in schools that serve historically underserved students, particularly students of color. Educators are being tasked with raising test scores, and high-stakes testing along with prepackaged curriculum is placing educators and students in a psychic prison.

In this compelling series we invite scholars and practitioners to address issues of diversity, equity, and social justice. The series seeks to provide books that will help educators to navigate the terrain of high-stakes testing that has resulted in the pedagogy of poverty. Drawing from critical multicultural education the series invites scholars and practitioners who have an interest in critical pedagogy, Critical Race Theory, antiracist education, religious diversity, critical theories in education, and social justice to provide practicing educators with knowledge to address the contemporary problems that have wreaked havoc on underserved students. This compelling series particularly speaks to practicing educators who hold positions as leaders, teachers, counselors, coaches, mentors, paraprofessionals, and others involved with student learning.

Titles in the Series

Perspectives on Diversity, Equity, and Social Justice in Educational Leadership, edited by Ashraf Esmail, Abul Pitre, and Antonette Aragon

Research Studies on Educating for Diversity and Social Justice, edited by Ashraf Esmail, Abul Pitre, Darren E. Lund, H. Prentice Baptiste, and Gwendolyn Duhon-Owens

English Language Learners: The Power of Culturally Relevant Pedagogies, edited by Ashraf Esmail, Abul Pitre, Alice Duhon Ross, Judith Blakely, and H. Prentice Baptiste

English Language Learners

The Power of Culturally Relevant Pedagogies

Edited by

Ashraf Esmail, Abul Pitre,
Alice Duhon Ross, Judith Blakely,
and H. Prentice Baptiste

ROWMAN & LITTLEFIELD
Lanham • Boulder • New York • London

Published by Rowman & Littlefield
An imprint of The Rowman & Littlefield Publishing Group, Inc.

4501 Forbes Boulevard, Suite 200, Lanham, Maryland 20706
www.rowman.com

86-90 Paul Street, London EC2A 4NE, United Kingdom

British Library Cataloguing in Publication Information Available

Library of Congress Cataloging-in-Publication Data Available

ISBN 9781475856149 (cloth : alk. paper) | ISBN 9781475856156 (pbk. : alk. paper) | ISBN 9781475856163 (epub)

∞™ The paper used in this publication meets the minimum requirements of American National Standard for Information Sciences—Permanence of Paper for Printed Library Materials, ANSI/NISO Z39.48-1992.

This book is dedicated to all teachers who work with English language learners. May you find the ultimate reward that working with these students can bring.

Contents

Acknowledgments

In 2012, a unique chapter in the history of NAME was forged when the series editors and Dr. Rose Duhon-Sells met with the Rowman & Littlefield team to finalize arrangements for the series. Under the visionary leadership of Dr. Rose Duhon-Sells, the NAME series became a reality, paving the way for transformative scholarship that could improve the quality of education in the United States and abroad for diverse student populations. The editors for this book are appreciative of the Rowman & Littlefield Education (RLE) division team: Tom Koerner, Carlie Wall, and Kira Hall. A special thanks to Nancy Evans, a former member of the RLE team who organized the initial meetings for the NAME series, and to Sarah Jubar for making the series a reality. The editors would like to thank all of the contributors to this volume for their interest and hard work on this important topic, English language learners.

Introduction

Toward Sustainable Culturally Responsive Pedagogies

Jancarlos J. Wagner-Romero

Language is the road map of a culture. It tells you where its people come from and where they are going.

—Rita Mae Brown

Imagine yourself in a classroom where all you hear are sounds, much like those heard from the teacher in many of the Charlie Brown movies. You try to make sense of them but find yourself squinting your eyes with confusion, hoping that someone will help you comprehend what is going on in the space that surrounds you. Laughter fills the air, yet you are unaware as to whether the sounds erupting from those around you are positive or done so in mockery of your inability to engage. So instead you sit there quietly, tuning out the diverse voices until someone is able to engage with you so that you, too, can make sense of what is happening and are able to laugh with purpose. Unfortunately, that someone does not come—or does so too late.

The experiences shared above resonate deeply for many English language learners, far too often than not. In a society where the social institution we all know to be "education" was built on whiteness and white supremacy, those with Limited English Proficiency (LEP) are often seen as the "other," thus causing them to fall through the cracks. No students, or parents for that matter, should feel helpless when all they want is a quality education that will prepare students for the realities they will face in our world—one that will prepare them for college or to engage in careers that will impact economic development and strengthen their upward mobility as human beings in a complex society.

From a lack of teacher training to the inability to recognize historical traumas faced by many non-English-speaking communities, students and families are faced with a harsh reality that leaves them wondering, "Can I make it in this system?" There is no doubt that those within "the system" have a responsibility to ensure that all students, no matter their linguistic abilities or cultural backgrounds, have the tools they need to thrive, and even more importantly, are afforded the opportunities that will set them on a path that dismantles the historical biases that have existed for far too long about this population. As educators, we must ask ourselves, "What can happen, though, when systems, schools, and educators implement culturally *responsive* pedagogies to better support this population of students?" "What might be the impact of these pedagogies if approached in ways that will ensure that they are *sustainable?*"

Non-English speakers continue to strengthen the makeup of educational spaces across the country, and it is no surprise that our schools are becoming increasingly diverse. Educators have the unique opportunity to build sustainable and socially just educational communities by engaging in culturally responsive pedagogies that are implemented with purpose. These pedagogies go far beyond celebrating a specific culture in a particular month of the year or hanging pictures of Brown people in a classroom as a means of demonstrating that representation matters.

Truly sustainable culturally responsive pedagogies disrupt deficit mindsets and challenge context-neutral thinking to ensure that students and the diversity they bring to an educational space are celebrated, appreciated, and used to drive educational experiences. Culturally responsive pedagogies go far beyond planning for instruction and rely heavily on shifts in mindsets in order to cultivate the skills and dispositions needed to best serve English language learners. In addition, culturally responsive pedagogies require the ability to cultivate authentic relationships with key stakeholders, find ways to engage the community at large, and come to the realization that the future of America—of the world—is multilingual and that language is deeply linked with human identity. As such, engaging in culturally responsive pedagogies cannot only be impactful for students and their families, but can be transformational for what is bound to be an increasingly global society.

As I reflect on my journey as an English language learner in the 1990s, from kindergarten through second grade, I cannot help but re-experience the shame that resonated through me day after day due to my inability to understand what was happening in the educational spaces around me. At the time, the term "culturally responsive pedagogy" was not something that educators were putting much emphasis on and, as a result, many of my peers dealt with navigating the same feelings I did: fear and shame. Sitting in the back of a classroom alone, or sometimes in a group of non-English-speaking peers, working on packets or listening to stories on cassette tapes were often the norm. While I eventually gained the fluency and comprehension skills necessary to test out of my English as a Second Language classes at the end of second grade, I transitioned to general education classrooms that still, for some reason, continued to cultivate a sense of shame.

Through reflection, I realized I never saw myself or people that looked like me or my family represented in day-to-day teaching and learning. There were very few times that we discussed pieces of literature about Latinx communities or engaged in meaningful conversations about the experiences of immigrant families. There is no doubt that these experiences are not unique to just myself. These are experiences that thousands upon thousands of young people have historically experienced—and continue to experience—in classrooms across the country.

As educators continue to grapple with the historical traumas of immigrant communities, acknowledging those truths can be a catalyst for reimagining what culturally responsive teaching and learning can look like. From my own experiences—personally as the son of immigrant parents whose native language is not English, and as an educator and scholar whose work has deeply focused on lifting the voices of my people and driving forth culturally sustaining practices for Limited English Proficient students—bringing to life truly equitable and culturally responsive pedagogies that are sustainable can and should be rooted in a number of things:

- Understanding that culture and language are directly tied to a young person's identity helps to pave the way for beyond-the-surface experiences for both teachers and their students. Who we are, where we come from, and the languages we speak *tell our truths*. Ignoring one's identity and truths is detrimental for so many reasons.
- Cultivating the mindsets, skills, and dispositions needed to meaningfully understand the complexities of a student's identity, as well as internalizing how intersectionality comes into play, are paramount to transforming the landscape of education for English language learners.
- Building and sustaining authentic relationships with students and their parents can lead to meaningful engagement from all parties. This includes learning about, understanding, and affirming culturally diverse experiences that lead to caring connections with those we serve.
- Engaging with community stakeholders, especially those doing critical advocacy work to advance the future of English language learners and Limited English Proficient families, creates a strong collaborative community with a common purpose. This requires countering the mindset

and common practice of working within the four walls of a classroom and being intentional about developing external partnerships that can have a positive, long-lasting impact on the lives of students and their families outside of the classroom environment.

- Moving from theory to practice, rooted in continuous coaching that leads to the implementation of culturally responsive pedagogies in the classroom and beyond, can help to shift the paradigm of the current landscape of education for English language learners. Think, "how can I move toward sustaining a culturally responsive and equitable environment for my English language learners?"

While I share valuable tenets that are important to me as a scholar and educator of English language learners, researchers and practitioners across the country have engaged in critical research for engaging in culturally responsive pedagogies that are sustainable—in other words, pedagogy that is long-lasting and transcends the surface-level culturally sensitive teaching and learning that many of us have been taught to pursue. In *Culturally Responsive Pedagogies for English Language Learners*, some of the field's most brilliant scholars focus on multifaceted approaches to culturally responsive pedagogies and their impacts on students and their communities. From working to understand how language influences human identity to reflecting on practices rooted in Social and Emotional Learning (SEL), this book serves as a critical tool for those who want to provide transformational experiences for English Language Learners.

Some might argue that education in America is at a turning point, especially after experiencing a global pandemic. One thing is for sure: how we engage English language learners—and how we meaningfully immerse ourselves in culturally responsive pedagogies *today*—will have a tremendous impact on the future of a community of students who, for far too long, have been kept on the sidelines of educational spaces.

Chapter 1

Providing Effective Learning Environments for English Learners through Practicing Care Theory and Understanding Identities

SoYoung Kang

As schools and classrooms become more diverse with the increasing number of English learners (ELs), educators focus more on inclusive education. Various strategies, such as differentiating instruction, are used by teachers to support and accommodate the needs of every student. Realizing students engage in learning more when the materials are culturally relevant, and using the problem-posing method or applying multicultural approaches, certainly impacts the comprehensible input and is important. However, providing effective learning environments for English learners through practicing care theory and understanding identities is even more essential.

As English learners face challenges in adjusting to a new culture and learning a new language, it is crucial for classroom teachers to understand the hardships of these students. It is not only the ELs who are experiencing challenges and culture shock, but also teachers who are struggling to understand that English learners go through similar phases.

CARE THEORY

Care theory plays an essential role in the school setting in relationship to epistemology due to the intimate relationship between how caring the teacher is and the knowledge that students gain. Human beings are socially constructed and influence one another in constructing knowledge. Noddings

(1984) argued that teaching should focus on the act of caring, and describes how teachers should care more about students than the content of instruction. In order to effectively care for students, teachers need to understand "what is happening in the family, the mass media, and the peer group, and how cultural and social trends are influencing the behaviors and ideas that students bring to the classroom" (Orstein & Levine, 2006, p. 288).

From an epistemological standpoint, emotions affect people as inquirers, because our emotions help us to choose what questions we want to address and try to understand (Thayer-Bacon & Bacon, 1998). Emotional feelings of caring are what motivate and inspire us. They can make us feel excited about learning.

Depending on how caring the teacher is and the other students are, students can improve their chances of becoming knowers. When people talk about someone being a knower, they tend to focus mainly on the pure knowledge they gain, instead of looking at the process of gaining knowledge. Care theory plays an essential role in the process of gaining knowledge, and everybody should pay attention to this process instead of only the resulting knowledge.

As an educator, encouraging people to realize the importance of care theory due to its relation with epistemology is critical, but what should be emphasized is valuing differences while the one caring and the one cared for engage in caring relationships. It will be problematic if the act of caring is examined only from the teacher's perspective instead of considering the students' perspectives, because there is no universal caring.

Caring is dependent on cultural or societal differences, and even more specifically on individual perspectives and interpretations. Similar to how every situation is different, everybody is different as well. Caring can never be viewed or defined in one way. One should always avoid limiting oneself by what was considered the norm in the past. Often, care theory has been generalized instead of specialized or considered in more specific terms. All humans are situated knowers, and it is important to identify who we are, where we are coming from, our backgrounds, and other variables. Taking the majority and applying the rules of majority to the minority is a real concern that should not be neglected.

COMMUNICATION

When people are communicating with each other, they tend to pay attention to the verbal messages and the most overt nonverbal messages (Meier & Davis, 2001). However, we have to always keep in mind that sometimes nonverbal expression can have richer information and the nature of nonverbal communication can be influenced by culture (Meier & Davis, 2001). In other words, when people talk about communication, they often focus on conversation or dialogical relations, but what we have to realize is that depending on cultures, the way or style of communication can vary enormously. We have to consider the diversity.

Communication can never be fully complete without both verbal and nonverbal elements. The poor relationship between teacher and student, between student and student, or among other human beings can lead people to relational poverty (Kang, 2008). Through cultural awareness of the students in the classroom and building positive relationships, the challenges that teachers experience could be reduced and transformed to a confidence in teaching and assisting English learners.

Communication without having cultural awareness, respect, and acceptance could lead to misunderstanding in relationships. Understanding other people's differences and uniqueness is as important as becoming aware of one's own cultural values, beliefs, and perceptions. Good communication skills are one of the most critical factors that one should have in caring relationships. Being aware of how communication is viewed differently in different countries should be recognized.

For example, depending on the culture, being silent does not mean that people are not communicating, but it is considered communicating in the "proper" way. If one talks too much in the classroom as a student, it might be viewed as being impolite or even challenging teachers. Since having good communication skills is one of the critical tools to have as a caring person, teachers need to be able to compare how good communication means different things cross-culturally.

CULTURE AND LANGUAGE

English learners experience challenges of a new culture and language. Having ELs in the classroom could also be challenging for the teachers. Communicating without having cultural awareness of the students could lead to misunderstanding. Learning and recognizing the individual differences could help teachers transform challenges to confidence.

In order to fully understand a culture, it is important to consider both surface and deep culture. Surface culture involves those aspects we easily notice as we interact with members of a culture, including visible aspects such as food, art, dress, holidays, and language. On the other hand, deep culture involves beliefs and values that cause the behaviors we see in members of a culture. Nontangible aspects of culture such as feelings, emotions, attitudes, and rules for interaction are seen at this level.

Language is the tool that people use to communicate, and constantly it transmits messages to people. It can be used to express emotions, and influence and control other people's behavior (Bloomfield, 1933). According to Whorf (1956), languages differ in their vocabularies and in their rules for combining words into sentences, and "these differences have cognitive and behavioral implications" (p. 121). Whorf also indicates that "speakers of widely differing languages not only speak about the world in different terms but actually experience the world in different ways" (p. 121). Thus, language has a great impact on human relationships.

As the number of immigrant families increases, it is commonly seen that the languages spoken by the family members are not limited to one language. Many people use two or more languages daily while belonging to one main culture. Since language and culture are interrelated, and language could be considered a part of culture, it would be beneficial for educators to explore the relationship between bilinguals and biculturals along with the issue of identity. In addition, as the differences in language have cognitive and behavioral implications, it is also important to realize that the speakers of widely differing languages not only speak about the world in different terms but also actually experience the world in different ways (Whorf, 1956).

IDENTITY

In order to provide an effective learning environment and best serve English learners, educators must first know about their students. It is important to have a good understanding of students' various backgrounds, including their first languages, previous educational background, and even about their families. Teachers can better respond to their students and support them in their learning if the struggles faced by students both in and outside of school are understood clearly (Freeman & Freeman, 2007).

People's identities are influenced by the various communities they belong to and are formed by interacting and relating with others. Young people construct their identities within embedded, diverse, and complex environments, a reflection of such elements as local political economy, peer relations, family circumstances, civic support, churches, schools, and neighborhood-based organizations (McLaughlin, 1993). Since people are constantly influenced by their context, it is important to understand the context of individuals in order to understand their identities.

To understand each individual, it is important to know that individual's distinctive culture. However, only looking at the culture and judging the personal can cause bias, since a cultural lens is not sufficient. Culture should be used as a tool to gather one aspect of information, but not all. As looking closely at each individual's identity will help a teacher understand the person and where he or she is coming from, to pay a great deal of attention to each individual's identity, more than just the culture would be required.

According to Foucault (1980), "The individual is not a pregiven entity which is seized on by the exercise of power. The individual, with his identity and characteristics, is the product of a relation of power exercised over bodies, multiplicities, movements, desires, forces" (p. 73). Since people are constantly influenced by their context, it is important to understand the context of people in order to understand their identities.

Another aspect of identity that we need to consider is the possibility of people having multiple identities. Everyone has multiple identities, and it is natural when one makes the important distinction between personal and social identity. One does not necessarily have to possess a single identity, but rather these multiple identities will help people adapt to different settings more easily with flexibility.

In observing identity, we also need to focus both on "the given identity" and "the formed identity." The given identity is something one is born with and that people have no choice in. It can be called "involuntary identity." For example, age, gender, place of birth, biological parents, color of skin are all factors that form one's identity involuntarily.

On the other hand, formed identity develops after birth, by oneself as well as by others. Formed identity is the identity that is "becoming," and it is more of a voluntary identity, although sometimes there is an involuntary quality to this as well since we learn through acculturation. People can form their own identity by interacting and relating with others. That is why it is important to look at culture in understanding people and in caring relationships. However, we have to avoid generalizing culture. It should be only used as a tool to understand and narrow down in gaining knowledge of individuals, since within each culture, there are many other subcultures as well (Kang, 2006).

THE POWER OF *BIBIMBAP* IN A DEMOCRATIC CLASSROOM: LANGUAGE AS A RESOURCE FOR ENGLISH LANGUAGE LEARNERS

Living in the United States, a society with such cultural diversity that it has been described as a salad bowl or tossed salad, it is significant for us to include diverse groups when we are applying certain skills or theories. In the past, instead of using the metaphor of a salad bowl, people used a melting pot (Nieto, 1992). It has changed to a salad bowl to see each ingredient or individual more distinctively rather than just mixing them together and seeing them as one. That is what we need to do for care theory as well.

As the number of English language learners rapidly increases in U.S. schools, teachers need to become more knowledgeable to work with non-English-speaking students. In assisting the ELs, instead of thinking of our world as a *juk* or *melting pot*, we need to rethink of it as a *bibimbap* or *tossed salad*. We should stop focusing on the issue of assimilation, but more on respecting each individual's uniqueness and strength.

Ruiz (1984) has described the historical development of three different orientations toward language: (1) language-as-a-handicap, which views ELLs as having a problem, even a handicap (1950s–1960s); (2) language-as-a-right— during the 1970s, the bilingual educators called for the rights of non-native English speakers to bilingual education; and (3) language-as-a-resource (more recent). For example, native English speakers also learn a second language, and they realize that the ELL students who are from different cultural backgrounds share many valuable resources.

In *Democracy and Education*, Dewey explained the importance of education as a social function and focused on how the school environment helps to develop the "immature" members of society. According to Dewey (1933), attitude is a critical element in reflective teaching and how individuals recognize and respond to problems. The emphasis is on open-mindedness, whole-heartedness, and responsibility. In today's diverse world, we need to reexamine who would be considered as the "immature." We have to realize that not only ELs but also anyone in the classroom could be considered immature. Everyone can help each other become better knowers in a democratic classroom/society, as Freire's (1970) problem-posing method of education emphasized the importance of a teacher and their students sharing power.

It is time to realize the importance of reexamining our diverse world as a bibimbap/tossed salad instead of a juk/melting pot. By setting a new perspective and focusing on language-as-a-resource, educators can effectively assist both English language learners and native English speakers to create a democratic classroom.

EDUCATIONAL IMPLICATIONS

As the diversity and the number of English learners visibly increase, the classroom can be full of students sharing different backgrounds of culture, race, gender, class, religion, and other variables. Having diverse students and understanding them will be another challenge for teachers, and teachers' role in educating children to live and work together respectfully is becoming more critical. Culturally relevant teachers also should not be hesitant to utilize students' culture as a vehicle for learning (Ladson-Billings, 1995). By understanding cultural pluralism and the importance of social relationships in this era, schools can certainly create a healthy classroom for all students.

In building up a caring relationship, communication and relational skills play essential roles. It is important that caring teachers not focus on helping English learners "adjust" or "adapt" to the teacher's culture or to the American culture only, but rather they should work on finding common ground for both teachers and students. If teachers try to explain and make students adjust to the teacher's own cultures and rules, students can become resistant and not even open up themselves to teachers.

English learners can feel uncomfortable and even offended in the relationship with teachers. The feeling can lead students to judge teachers as someone who does not understand them, and students can eventually draw back from teachers, which could also negatively influence students learning. Instead of imposing teachers' value, listening to English learners should come first.

Without understanding where English learners are coming from, it will be difficult for the teacher to effectively help them. Teachers must understand identities are influenced by the various communities English learners belong to, and they are formed by interacting and relating with others. Through practicing care theory and recognizing identities, teachers can certainly provide effective learning environments for English learners in their classroom.

REFERENCES

Bloomfield, L. (1933). *Language*. Holt, Rinehart & Winston.

Dewey, J. (1933). *How we think: A restatement of the relation of reflective thinking to the educative process*. D.C. Heath & Co.

Foucault, M. (1980). *Power/knowledge: Selected interviews and other writings, 1972–1977* (Colin Gordon, Ed.; Colin Gordon et al., Trans.). Pantheon Books.

Freeman, D., & Freeman, Y. (2007). *English language learners: The essential guide*. Scholastic.

Freire, P. (1970). *Pedagogy of the oppressed* (M. Bergman Ramos, Trans.). Seabury Press.

Kang, S. (2006). Identity-centered multicultural care theory: White, black, and Korean caring. *Educational Foundations, 20*, 3–4.

Kang, S. (2008). Relational poverty: Enrichment through care theory. In F. Godwyll & S. Kang (Eds.), *Poverty, education and development* (pp. 125–133). Nova Science Publishers.

Ladson-Billings, G. (1995). Toward a theory of culturally relevant pedagogy. *American Educational Research Journal, 32*(3), 465–491.

McLaughlin, M. (1993). What matters most in teachers' workplace context. In Judith Warren Little & Milbrey McLaughlin (Eds.), *Teachers' work: Individuals, colleagues, and contexts*. Teachers College Press.

Meier, S., & Davis, S. R. (2001). *The elements of counseling.* Brooks/Cole.

Nieto, S. (1992). *Affirming diversity: The sociopolitical context of multicultural education.* Longman.

Noddings, N. (1984). *Caring: A feminine approach to ethics and moral education.* University of California Press.

Orstein, A. C., and Levine, D. U. (2006). *Foundations of education.* Houghton Mifflin Company.

Ruiz, R. (1984). Orientations in language planning. *Journal of the National Association for Bilingual Education, 8*(2), 15–34.

Thayer-Bacon, B., & Bacon, C. (1998). *Philosophy applied to education: Nurturing a democratic community in the classroom.* Prentice-Hall.

Whorf, B. L. (1956). *Language, thought, and reality: Selected writings of Benjamin Lee Whorf* (J. B. Carroll, Ed.). MIT Press.

Chapter 2

Moving Toward Coherent and Collaborative Coaching for Linguistically Responsive Teaching

Monica S. Yoo, Leslie Grant, Lisa Fetman, and Veronica Garza

> I feel like it's been really positive and it's really just helped me grow in an area where I felt really unsure. I feel like I've grown a lot in my confidence teaching my language learners.

The quote above from Anna, a veteran teacher, notes how sustained coaching can make a difference in providing professional development for K–12 teachers who are working with culturally and linguistically diverse learners. This chapter focuses on the coaching received by two in-service teachers (ISTs), Anna and Samuel, who are earning a culturally and linguistically diverse education (CLDE) endorsement.

As not all K–12 teachers have access to working with coaches who have received training related to teaching English learners (ELs), this chapter explores (a) the successes and challenges related to the coaching of two secondary teachers and (b) the applications for teachers in a broader school context, with ideas for peer collaboration and possible implementation of aspects of a CLDE coaching intervention, with or without a coach.

RELEVANT BACKGROUND LITERATURE

Research has revealed that coaching can positively lead to more effective instruction (Matsumura et al., 2013; Sailors & Price, 2015; Teemant, 2014) and improvements in student achievement (Bean et al., 2010; Elish-Piper & L'Allier, 2011; Matsumura et al., 2013). More specifically, the literature on coaching teachers of ELs, though limited, has addressed combining professional development (PD) with sustained coaching. Batt (2010) and Song (2016) found that teachers were more likely to put into practice English as a Second Language (ESL) structures and strategies when they had both PD based on the Sheltered Instruction Observation Protocol (SIOP) (Echevarria et al., 2017)—a set of research-based practices *and* strategies known to be beneficial in learning English as well as academic content—*and* coaching, as compared to PD alone.

While results from these studies are favorable, Lucas and Villegas (2010) argued that ISTs need more PD focused on linguistically responsive teaching, which not only outlines skills for more effective teaching but also underscores fostering an awareness of the larger sociocultural and sociopolitical context of teaching. They encourage the development of *orientations, knowledge,* and *skills* through linguistically responsive-focused PD in order to guide ISTs away from a "deficit" mindset to one that values ELs' cultural and linguistic assets.

Although the coaching literature is fairly extensive, research on specific activities that lead to teachers' instructional changes, and why these activities have been chosen, has been less clear. Thus, researchers have examined the literature on high-quality teacher PD to identify elements related to improving practice for impact on student learning (Desimone & Pak, 2017; Gibbons & Cobb, 2017). Key elements from the PD literature that overlap with the coaching literature have been distilled in a framework by Desimone and Pak (2017), which includes *collective participation, content focus, active learning, duration, and coherence.*

In particular, this chapter will unpack and explore the concept of *coherence* in greater depth compared to other areas of the framework, as this conceptual category, in connection with some of the others, can be invaluable for examining the growth and development of ISTs. PD through coaching is most likely to have a positive impact when it aligns or coheres with teachers' goals, knowledge, and beliefs; content; context; curriculum; and school and district policies (Desimone & Pak, 2017). Walqui (2019) further notes that *coherence* through scaffolded learning opportunities for English learners needs to be woven across micro (task), meso (lesson), and macro (unit) levels. Coaches need to support and help teachers apply what they've learned in order to create instructional changes that will last.

THE COACHES AND TEACHERS

The ISTs *collectively participated* (Desimone & Pak, 2017) in a cohort with six others who were likewise receiving coaching and taking university coursework. Both language knowledge (Bunch, 2013) and disciplinary expertise (Di Domenico et al., 2018) brought by the coach and IST jointly provided a *content focus* to the ISTs' coaching/PD as they engaged in *active learning* (Desimone & Pak, 2017) by reflecting on their teaching and analyzing EL student work (Hasbrouck, 2017).

The *duration* (Desimone & Pak, 2017) consisted of over 24 hours via eight coaching cycles (CC1–CC8) over 2 years—well beyond a 20-hour minimum required for sustained PD (Garet et al., 2001). Each cycle consisted of a pre-conference, observation, and post-conference, and an examination of student work. The ISTs were also interviewed about coaching at the end of the program.

Janice and James, the coaches, were experienced educators with training and experience working with ELs. Both were attuned to language learners' needs. Janice had been a foreign language teacher, and James had taught ELs in the United States and abroad. They implemented a university-created protocol, while tapping into their CLDE expertise. The protocol's prompts included questions such as: "How will students demonstrate their learning?" (pre) and "What did you notice about your students, including ELs, and their learning during the lesson?" (post).

By engaging ISTs in active reflection on EL student work and conversations about diverse learners' needs (i.e., discussing academic language, comprehensible input, and other SIOP-related components), the coaches successfully guided the development of ISTs' views and instruction for ELs. However, the ISTs still were left with challenges. The examples provided in this chapter relate to interactions between Janice and Samuel, a first-year teacher in social studies, and James and Anna, an 11-year veteran IST in English language arts (ELA).

During the study, Samuel taught American history and economics at an urban high school that served a racially, ethnically, and socioeconomically diverse population. All of his classes contained a number of ELs of varying levels of proficiency. Anna taught ELA at a suburban middle school fairly close to a military base that was socioeconomically, but not as racially and ethnically, diverse. In contrast to Samuel, Anna had very few ELs in her classes.

SUCCESSES

The successes experienced by the ISTs reflected their growth in becoming linguistically responsive (Lucas & Villegas, 2010). As reflected in Anna's quote earlier in the chapter, both she and Samuel felt "unsure" about working with ELs when they first began the CLDE program. However, they both grew in their understanding of ELs as they reflected with their coaches.

Foundational to being a linguistically responsive educator is knowing who ELs are, including their strengths, assets, and linguistic abilities. ISTs must examine their beliefs and orientations regarding ELs (Lucas & Villegas, 2010). Anna, in her end-of-year interview, explained,

> I've realized that . . . our language learners deserve to hold on to their native language—their L1—and to learn English is not about being an English speaker, it's about being bilingual. . . . Language learners should not be treated the same as our students on IEPs. . . . Accommodations and modifications . . . that we use for language learners are different.

Her change in perspective, along with her newly acquired knowledge of second language learning (Lucas & Villegas, 2010), was reflected in how she zeroed in on a particular student.

She began to understand his hesitancy to speak and became attuned to his language needs regarding how to structure questions. She then provided him with opportunities for participating in class with grammatical structures that could build his confidence. Implementing such structures for this student expanded her skillset (Lucas & Villegas, 2010) as a teacher of ELs.

Similarly, coaching impacted Samuel's thinking about how to scaffold instruction for ELs. He noted,

> The coaching cycles encouraged me to reflect . . . on what I am doing to better help EL students. . . . They encouraged me to be more visual and thorough with things like coaching and modeling. . . . [I] understand that although I do a lot of these things, there's always more that I could do.

As a beginning teacher, the strategies learned from his coursework and coaching helped him to build skills related to differentiating instruction for ELs. He also realized that there could never be an endpoint to professional learning and growth as a teacher.

CHALLENGES

Despite coaching successes, we found gaps in *coherence* (Desimone & Pak, 2017) that resulted in missed opportunities for prompting ISTs to fully enact linguistically responsive teaching (Lucas & Villegas, 2010). As Samuel and Janice reviewed students' work in coaching cycle 1 (CC1), Samuel puzzled over why some students with higher language proficiency "missed" the answers, while others with lower proficiency did not. Janice commented that economics is more "conceptual versus concrete," and advocated that he use fewer words and more visuals.

However, Janice did not provide concrete ideas regarding *when* a visual could aid in teaching particular economic concepts. Although Samuel added more visuals over time, these additions may not have "cohered" with his experiences, as he pondered, "What I'm always looking for is: Am I doing enough of that [visual support]? Where could I be doing more of it? And . . . are [the visuals] relevant? . . . Applicable? . . . Are the visuals I'm using actually working?" (CC4).

While adopting this skill-expanding strategy was a "success" for Samuel, he still found it to be challenging. He noted in various instances that he was unsure whether or not students were "getting" particular abstract concepts. Although he perceived the implementation of visuals to be helpful in teaching American history, he had difficulty applying this to economics.

A coaching conversation between Anna and James in CC7 further illustrates a missed opportunity for teacher learning. Anna, discussing a student's Socratic seminar response, stated, "[The student] did try to make his own question; it's not necessarily grammatically correct, but I can tell what he was trying to ask." James suggested that Anna create a separate graphic organizer to help the student with the grammatical structure. This led to Anna's "success" in implementing a new strategy for the one student.

However, James did not have Anna think through *how* she might incorporate such a strategy into her teaching with a class of mostly monolingual English speakers and a few ELs. So while she was developing her skills in this area, she was not sure how to apply them beyond the work with one individual.

Commenting on the same Socratic seminar, Anna reflected, "I wish the students were more conversational. . . . The discussions felt fairly stiff. . . . I would still like for students to be more comfortable using . . . academic and formal language." What she wanted to accomplish with the class was at odds with her plans for the individual. This left her with a strategy that wasn't easily going to "cohere," as it was decontextualized from the curriculum and her classroom. Could the coach not have led her to create grammatical structures for questioning, while also having the student, along with others, find ways to sound more natural in an academic setting?

WHAT CAN BE LEARNED FROM
MISSED OPPORTUNITIES?

The coaches could have encouraged the ISTs to build on their in-the-moment learning to formulate next steps leading to greater coherence across current and future lessons. Both ISTs grappled with addressing ELs' language needs and could have used more guidance in order to connect language-learning practices to their disciplinary contexts. Coaching could have helped (but may not have) to strengthen the connections between content, active learning, and coherence. While the ISTs wanted to pursue these connections, the coaches were not necessarily attuned to them.

Teachers who work effectively with ELs must consider how to enhance their lessons with cooperative structures and scaffolds that will make the challenging content accessible, all the while supporting language development, along with the needs of individuals and the class. While the ISTs and coaches in this study clearly focused on teachers' repertoire of skills to address the needs of ELs, this was often applied only at the micro (task) level, rather than taking into account the fit of skills and strategies across meso (lesson) and macro (unit) levels of instruction (Walqui, 2019), the curriculum, and the fit with school and district policies (Desimone & Pak, 2017).

ENACTING COACHING-LIKE
STRUCTURES WITHIN A SCHOOL

Resources, such as PD with exemplary consultants, videos featuring nationally recognized CLDE educators, participation in state and national TESOL organizations, accessing of internet resources recommended by TESOL, and book studies using published research and best practices can all support in-school efforts to improve instruction for ELs by providing models and guidance for teachers. These resources, along with regularly scheduled meetings over an academic year, could function as starting places to begin and sustain conversations among a *collective* group of ISTs within a school (Desimone & Pak, 2017).

Teachers with CLDE experience can serve as teacher partners/mentors, in lieu of coaches. Providing partner/mentor teams with guiding questions, such as the examples from the coaching protocol, can assist in helping ISTs identify areas, such as academic language, discourse, cultural and linguistic differences, and so on, that could be challenging for ELs. ISTs at the same school could be provided release time in order to observe and learn from one another. ISTs also might record their lessons and share with colleagues for targeted feedback.

In addition, ISTs can set aside time to examine and discuss the work of students who are at various stages of learning English in order to identify and address students' specific needs. Colleagues within the same school, rather than coaches from the outside, likely will be more able to reflect on and discuss ways to create coherence in relation to instruction, the curriculum, and the context. Such efforts could provide ongoing sustained PD (Desimone & Pak, 2017).

In line with the framework by Desimone and Pak (2017), these collaborative, school-based, coaching-like structures can enable coherence in teacher development, while establishing culturally and linguistically responsive instruction for all students.

REFERENCES

Batt, E. G. (2010). Cognitive coaching: A critical phase in professional development to implement sheltered instruction. *Teaching and Teacher Education, 26*(4), 997–1005. https://doi:10.1016/j.tate.2009.10.042

Bean, R. M., Draper, J. A., Hall, V., Vandermolen, J., & Zigmond, N. (2010). Coaches and coaching in Reading First schools: A reality check. *The Elementary School Journal, 111*(1), 87–114. http://doi:10.1086/653471

Bunch, G. C. (2013). Pedagogical language knowledge: Preparing mainstream teachers for English learners in the new standards era. *Review of Research in Education, 37*(1), 298–341. http://doi:10.3102/0091732X12461772

Desimone, L. M., & Pak, K. (2017). Instructional coaching as high-quality professional development. *Theory Into Practice, 56*(1), 3–12. https://www.tandfonline.com/doi/abs/10.1080/00405841.2016.1241947

Di Domenico, P. M., Elish-Piper, L., Manderino, M., & L'Allier, S. K. (2018). Coaching to support disciplinary literacy instruction: Navigating complexity and challenges for sustained teacher change. *Literacy Research and Instruction, 57*(2), 81–99. http://doi:10.1080/19388071.2017.1365977

Echevarria, J., Vogt, M., & Short, D. (2017). *Making content comprehensible for English learners: The SIOP model* (5th ed.). Pearson.

Elish-Piper, L., & L'Allier, S. K. (2011). Examining the relationship between literacy coaching and student reading gains in grades K–3. *The Elementary School Journal, 112*(1), 83–106. https://doi.org/10.1086/660685

Garet, M. S., Porter, A. C., Desimone, L., Birman, B. F., & Yoon, K. S. (2001). What makes professional development effective? Results from a national sample of teachers. *American Educational Research Journal, 38*(4), 915–945. doi:10.3102/00028312038004915

Gibbons, L. K., & Cobb, P. (2017). Focusing on teacher learning opportunities to identify potentially productive coaching activities. *Journal of Teacher Education, 68*(4), 411–425. https://doi.org/10.1177/0022487117702579

Hasbrouck, J. (2017). Student-focused coaching. *Theory Into Practice, 56*(1), 21–28. http://doi:10.1080/00405841.2016.1252219

Lucas, T., & Villegas, A. (2010). The missing piece in teacher education: The preparation of linguistically responsive teachers. *National Society for the Study of Education, 109*(2), 297–318.

Matsumura, L. C., Garnier, H. E., & Spybrook, J. (2013). Literacy coaching to improve student reading achievement: A multi-level mediation model. *Learning and Instruction, 25*, 35–48. https://doi.org/10.1016/j.learninstruc.2012.11.001

Sailors, M., & Price, L. (2015). Support for the improvement of practices through intensive coaching (SIPIC): A model of coaching for improving reading instruction and reading achievement. *Teaching and Teacher Education, 45*, 115–127. https://doi.org/10.1016/j.tate.2014.09.008

Song, K. H. (2016). Systematic professional development training and its impact on teachers' attitudes toward ELLs: SIOP and guided coaching. *TESOL Journal, 7*(4), 767–799. http://doi:10.1002/tesj.240

Teemant A. (2014). A mixed-methods investigation of instructional coaching for teachers of diverse learners. *Urban Education, 49*(5), 574–604. http://doi:10.1177/0042085913481362

Walqui, A. (2019). Designing the amplified lesson. In A. Walqui & G. C. Bunch (Eds.), *Amplifying the curriculum: Designing quality learning opportunities for English Learners* (pp. 43–70). Teachers College Press.

Chapter 3

Working with Undocumented Immigrant Students

Developing and Sustaining Longstanding Relationships

James Cohen, Magdalena Haro, Sarah
Heinz, and Thalia Marron

Illegal immigrants! Wetbacks! Aliens! All derogatory words associated with a person without documentation who enters the territory of the United States. The authors of this chapter argue that these terms are dehumanizing and instead prefer to use the term *undocumented immigrant*, or as the Pew Research Center and Migration Policy Institute often use, *unauthorized immigrant*. People cannot be illegal; everyone has the right to exist. People, however, *can* be without documentation or unauthorized to be in a certain location (i.e., in the United States without papers).

Calling undocumented immigrants "illegal aliens" reenforces a mindset that allows for the continuance of locking up children in giant dog cages in remodeled Wal-Marts on the southern border without much uproar from the general populace because, of course, they are illegal (don't have the right to be here). Moreover, few Americans think twice about the separation of families because the people who are coming across the border are "aliens" (thought of as subhuman or even nonhumans).

To have conversations about undocumented immigration with certain individuals who buy into this belief system, and to hear the derogatory terms they use on a regular basis, it is clear that they are very quick to blame the victim: "They shouldn't be here in the first place"; "they deserve to be locked up and separated from their parents/kids because they broke the law."

The purpose of this chapter is not to blame the migrant, but instead to provide perspective regarding the estimated 11.3 million undocumented immigrants and more specifically the 1.09 million undocumented students in our schools by providing facts about the realities of this group of people. Both the media and Democratic and Republican administrations over the years have spread untruths about undocumented immigrants for the purpose of instilling fear to control the populace and obtain votes.

They make claims that undocumented immigrants are here to pillage our economy and our institutions (e.g., health and education, etc.), commit crimes of rape (of White women) and rob businesses, and destroy the American cultural and societal fabric *en masse*. These mistruths feed into xenophobic beliefs exacerbating both ire and stress for the believer as well as adding stress, pain, and inequities to the undocumented immigrants themselves.

In other words, the authors of this chapter argue that educators must know the truth about undocumented immigrants to take one step closer to American society becoming more accepting and open to the human beings sitting in the seats in front of them in their respective classrooms and schools. By being more accepting, all parties will benefit.

People who believe in the mistruths can potentially reduce their anger against this population because they will learn the facts of undocumented immigrants being here. Moreover, the undocumented immigrants themselves will also benefit because they will receive less hatred and ire from society, schools and teachers.

In this chapter, the authors first deliver the demographics by asking, *Who are undocumented immigrants in the United States?* This is followed with the issues undocumented immigrant students face while they are in the U.S. PK–12 system. The chapter ends with suggestions for how to most productively and effectively work with undocumented students.

NUMBERS, INFLUENCE ON ECONOMY, AND EDUCATIONAL LEVELS

In 2018, there were 11.2 million undocumented immigrants living in the United States, representing nearly every country that exists in the world. Of the 11.2 million, the top countries represented are Mexico at 25%, China at 6%, India at 6%, the Philippines at 4%, and El Salvador at 3% (Budiman, 2020). From 2010 to 2017, the numbers of undocumented immigrants shifted tremendously.

Mexicans had a reduction of 50,000, and undocumented immigrants from India (+265,000) and Venezuela (+80,000) grew more than any other country. The countries with the largest population decline during this 7-year period (in addition to Mexico) were: Philippines (–70,000), Ecuador (–45,000), and Korea (–40,000) (Warren, 2019; Center for Migration Studies, 2017). And contrary to popular belief, the majority (62%) of undocumented immigrants did not cross the southern border with Mexico, but instead came to the United States legally and overstayed their visas (Warren, 2017). The remaining 38% did indeed cross the southern border with Mexico.

Despite the plethora of misinformation in society regarding undocumented immigrants (e.g., don't pay taxes, destroy our economy), undocumented individuals contribute more to the U.S. economy than the media or politicians let on. According to the American Immigration Council (2020), in 2018 undocumented immigrants contributed $20.1 billion in taxes.

This is significant considering that if the American government were to deport all undocumented immigrants, not only would the U.S. economy lose those tax dollars, but it would also have to pay approximately $10,070 for each deportation (Wolgin, 2015), or $112.8 billion to remove all undocumented immigrants.

Like the regular American-born population, undocumented immigrants' education levels vary widely. Although undocumented immigrants are three times as likely to not have had completed high school compared to their U.S. born peers (27% vs. 8%) (Budiman, 2020), the latest data suggest that of the high school graduates, undocumented immigrants are as likely as the U.S. born to have a bachelor's degree or more (32% and 33%) (Budiman, 2020). In fact, new estimates indicate that there are over 450,000 undocumented immigrants attending some form of postsecondary education, making up approximately 2% of all postsecondary students (Presidents' Alliance on Higher Education and Immigration, 2020).

ISSUES TO THINK ABOUT IN THE CLASSROOM/SCHOOL

Some of the main issues that undocumented immigrant students experience include psychological, emotional, and physical manifestations of stress, which often create a context in which their academic success struggles (Chavarria et al., 2021). The xenophobic, anti-immigrant, racist, and anti-Muslim rhetoric from the 2016 presidential campaign coupled with the heightened deportation and rapid immigration policy changes marking the first years of the Trump administration. As a result, PK–12 students of immigrant origin experienced fear, anxiety, difficulty concentrating, bullying, and hateful speech from peers (Costello, 2016; Gándara & Ee, 2018; Rogers et al., 2017).

This rhetoric did not stop, however. Along with the scapegoating of immigrants and asylum seekers added to the 400+ anti-immigrant executive orders signed over the 4 years of the Trump administration, students in PK–12 schools across the country continued to experience hateful commentary and bullying from their peers.

As an example of this hateful commentary, in one diverse middle school in the Midwest, to the dismay of teachers, administrators, and children alike, a child was seen/heard building a wall of backpacks in the school cafeteria during lunch, exclaiming at the top of his lungs, "Mexicans need to go home! We need to build a wall!" This type of rhetoric was clearly borrowed from President Trump and his supporters' incessant repetition of these pithy hateful memes.

Unfortunately, when children hear such commentary and vocally repeat it, whether they fully understand it or not, it instills fear and trepidation in the undocumented students in earshot of this commentary as well as creates a chilling factor in the school. Needless to say, expositions like this are hate speech and do not belong in any school.

Another example is demonstrated in a study conducted by Figueroa (2017) in which she interviewed undocumented fifth-grade students and inquired when they decided to share or withhold their status and how this impacted their educational settings. The results revealed that students who obtained resident status were open and willing to share their border-crossing stories with classmates.

However, the undocumented students avoided participation in classroom activities, especially in the socioemotional lessons that focused on identity exploration. Undocumented students were afraid to share personal information because of fear of getting themselves or their family members deported. Many of these students were instructed by their parents to not talk to anyone about their status, which caused some students to lie and say that they were born in the United States.

In contrast, students are often told by their teachers to be honest and proud of who they are, thus creating an internal dilemma. Do the students tell the truth of their immigration status and thus go against their parents' wishes, or do they stay quiet and go against the ultimate authority figure in the classroom? This conflict can create a disconnect with their self-identity, resulting in those students not participating in class.

They start becoming labeled as "the quiet one" or "the shy one" and critiqued as "she doesn't want to learn," "he is not motivated," or "she doesn't care." Unfortunately, the reality of the above context combined with the constant and ongoing threat of deportation creates a situation of worry and anxiety that frequently keeps students living in the shadows (Todd et al., 2020).

Researchers have argued that exposure to traumatic events can lead to further challenges for undocumented students and families seeking to create a life and obtain an education in the United States (Booi et al., 2016). In addition to the political rhetoric they experience once in the United States, the undocumented students' crossing into the United States is often extremely traumatic. They witness rapes, murders, and death and can be left behind if they cannot keep up with the coyote guiding them across the desert (De Leon, 2015). If they do make it across, the policies implemented by the Trump administration create an even more precarious situation.

As an example, Carlos is an 11-year-old student in the fifth grade. He crossed the border with his family and entered the United States from Mexico. Carlos and his family fled Mexico to escape increasing levels of violence and instability. Upon crossing the border, Carlos was separated from his family due to the Trump administration's zero-tolerance immigration policy.

It took approximately two months before Carlos was finally reunited with his parents (Crawford et al., 2017). As a result of these traumatic events, Carlos has trouble focusing on assignments and keeps falling asleep during class. Traumatic events such as these can adversely affect the social, emotional, and mental well-being of students, which can directly affect their ability to learn (Connery, 2018).

In addition to the issues explicated above, it is common for undocumented students to have teachers who hold on to assimilationist ideologies. The assimilationist paradigm is the belief that when immigrants come to the United States, they should drop their language, their culture, and their beliefs and pick up English and become an "American" (whatever being "an American" means to the holder of this belief system).

Teachers with this mindset expect students to speak English on their first day in the classroom, not considering what they have been through (Rodriguez et al., 2018) or the fact that it takes a minimum of 4 to 7 years to learn academic English (Witt et al., 2000). This expectation by the teacher positions the student as intellectually and culturally inferior and systematically erodes any semblance of self-worth (Nieto & Bode, 2018; Valenzuela, 1999).

CLASSROOM AND SCHOOL SUGGESTIONS

Whether teachers have an undocumented student in their classroom or not, their presence in school still impacts teachers and their students in various ways (Migration Policy Institute, 2020). In some cases, your students have a friend who is undocumented; this can impact your students' psychological well-being due to worry of losing their friend to deportation.

The teacher teaching next door to you has an undocumented immigrant in her classroom; this can potentially affect the content or dynamics of the classroom environment. Due to this, it is imperative that all teachers are educated with the knowledge to assist in providing the most effective and productive classroom environment.

The authors provide three broad principles in this section on how an educator can best teach and collaborate with undocumented students. These practices are to be modified based on the type of student, classroom, and community that one works with on a daily basis.

The first principle for educators is keeping oneself up to date about current policies, the political climate, and outside adversities that may create or enhance students' fear of deportation or being separated from their family. A teacher of a diverse group of students should be aware of how the current temperament of society may impact their students socially and emotionally. In schools, teachers are able to provide a loving, caring, culturally respectful environment, but outside of the four walls of their classrooms, undocumented students may experience a wide variety of personal hardships such as socio-economic struggles, family relationship adversity, and xenophobia on a daily basis (Cholera et al., 2020).

The political climate that entails ever-changing, stress-inducing anti-immigration policies in combination with such personal adversity make for a perfect storm of grief for the student. This may result in social and academic deficits in the classroom. Therefore, it behooves teachers to be understanding and educated about such events and perspectives so that they are not only able to be there for those students in times of fear and hurt, but also able to understand a bit more of what the students are feeling and why.

After taking steps to educate themselves about the current climate, the second principle is to form a well-nurtured personal and trusting relationship with their undocumented students. As good teachers would do with all their students, if allowable by the student, get to know what kind of person they truly are. By being genuine and allowing that student to take the time and feel comfortable being around a school professional, a trusting relationship can be formed.

Once a relationship is formed, a deeper understanding of student needs is more easily accessible. This knowledge can lead to the ability to seek out resources for the students and their families and can demonstrate that the teacher has their best interests at heart. Providing students an environment where they feel comfortable reaching out to the teacher about certain emotions or fears they may have and responding with words of comfort or resources (e.g., a referral to the school counselor) can lead to more interactions that show a trusting interpersonal connection/professional student-teacher relationship (U.S. Department of Education [USDE], 2015). This connection can help reduce the fear that students and families frequently have of school personnel.

A final principle for educators working with undocumented students is being an advocate. Students who come from undocumented and mixed-status households often refrain from reaching out to their school when they are in need (USDE, 2015). Whether it be a linguistic barrier, attendance conflict, or a social or cultural issue, it is imperative that educators maintain constant, explicit communication with families, reach out to other school faculty/ professionals if they cannot provide the proper resources or information, and consistently connect with undocumented students, utilizing that trusting, personal relationship that has been built.

Forming that critical relationship with an undocumented student and their family will allow teachers to advocate for them and be able to provide their children with the most productive and effective learning and social possibilities, both in and outside the classroom.

REFERENCES

American Immigration Council. (2020, August). *Immigrants in the United States.* https://www.americanimmigrationcouncil.org/research/immigrants-in-the-united -states

Booi, Z., Callahan, C., Fugere, G., Harris, M., Hughes, A., Kramarczuk, A., Kurtz, C., Reyes, R., & Swaminathan, S. (2016). Ensuring every undocumented student succeeds: A report on access to public education for undocumented children. Georgetown Law Human Rights Institute Fact-Finding Project. https://www .urban-response.org/system/files/content/resource/files/main/public-education-for -undocumented-children.pdf

Budiman, A. (2020, August). *Key findings about U.S. immigrants.* Pew Research Center. https://www.pewresearch.org/fact-tank/2020/08/20/key-findings-about-u-s -immigrants

Center for Migration Studies. (2017). *Venezuela in crisis: The plight of Venezuelan refugees.* https://cmsny.org/venezuela-in-crisis

Chavarria, K., Cornejo, M., Ayón, C., & Enriquez, L.E. (2021). Disrupted education?: A latent profile analysis of immigration-related distractions and academic engagement among undocumented college students. *Journal of Latinos and Education, 20*(3), 232–245. https://doi.org/10.1080/15348431.2021.1949989

Cholera, R., Falusi, O. O., & Linton, J. M. (2020). Sheltering in place in a xenophobic climate: COVID-19 and children in immigrant families. *Pediatrics, 146*(1), e20201094. doi:10.1542/peds.2020–1094

Connery, C. (2018). *Issue brief: The impact of undocumented status on children's learning.* NEAG School of Education.

Costello, M. (2016). *The Trump effect: The impact of the presidential campaign in our nation's schools.* Southern Poverty Law Center.

Crawford, E. R., Aguayo, D., & Valle, F. (2017). Counselors as leaders who advocate for undocumented students' education. *Journal of Research on Leadership Education, 14*(2), 119–150.

De Leon, J. (2015). *The land of open graves: Living and dying on the migrant trail.* University of California Press.

Figueroa, M. A. (2017). Speech or silence: Undocumented students' decisions to disclose or disguise their citizenship status in school. *American Educational Research Journal, 54*(3), 485–523.

Gándara, P., & Ee, J. (2018). *U.S. immigration enforcement policy and its impact on teaching and learning in the nation's schools* (Working paper). The Civil Rights Project/Proyecto Derechos Civiles.

Migration Policy Institute. (2020, October 1). Profile of the unauthorized population—US. Retrieved November 08, 2020, from https://www.migrationpolicy.org/data/unauthorized- immigrant-population/state/US

Nieto, S., & Bode, P. (2018). *Affirming diversity: The sociopolitical context of multicultural education* (7th ed.). Pearson.

Presidents' Alliance on Higher Education and Immigration. (2020). *Undocumented students in higher education: How many students are in U.S. colleges and universities, and who are they?* https://www.presidentsalliance.org/wp-content/uploads/2020/07/Undocumented-Students-in-Higher-Education-April-2020.pdf

Rodriguez, S., Monreal, T., & Howard, J. (2018): "It's about hearing and understanding their stories": Teacher empathy and socio-political awareness toward newcomer undocumented students in the New Latino South. *Journal of Latinos and Education, 19*(2), 181–198. doi:10.1080/15348431.2018.1489812

Rogers, J., Franke, M., Yun, J. E., Ishimoto, M., Diera, C., Geller, R., Berryman, A., & Brenes, T. (2017). *Teaching and learning in the age of Trump: Increasing stress and hostility in America's high schools.* UCLA's Institute for Democracy, Education, and Access.

Todd, A., Ayala, C., & Barraza, K. (2020). School counselors working with undocumented students in K–12 school settings. *Journal of School Counseling, 18*(14).

U.S. Department of Education. (2015). *Supporting undocumented youth resource guide.* National Center on Safe Supportive Learning Environments. Retrieved October 20, 2015, from https://www2.ed.gov/about/overview/focus/supporting-undocumented-youth.pdf

Valenzuela, A. (1999). *Subtractive schooling: U.S.–Mexican youth and the politics of caring.* SUNY Press.

Warren, R. (2017). DHS overestimates visa overstays for 2016; overstay population growth near zero during the year. *Journal on Migration and Human Security, 5*(4), 768–779. https://doi.org/10.1177/233150241700500403

Warren, R. (2019). US undocumented population continued to fall from 2016 to 2017, and visa overstays significantly exceeded illegal crossings for the seventh consecutive year. *Journal on Migration and Human Security, 7*(1), 19–22.

Witt, D., Hakuta, K., & Butler, Y. (2000). *How long does it take English learners to attain proficiency?* University of California, Linguistic Minority Research Institute.

Wolgin, P. E. (2015). What would it cost to deport all 5 million beneficiaries of executive action on immigration? Center for American Progress. https://www .americanprogress.org/issues/immigration/news/2015/02/23/106983/what-would -it-cost-to-deport-all-5-million-beneficiaries-of-executive-action-on-immigration/ ?_ga=2.137064496.1019958034.1633915309-364442015.1633915309

Chapter 4

Assessing the English Language Learner

Amy Van Buren

Assessment of English language learners (ELLs) impacts all phases of their academic lives, from initial identification of needs to academic progress and throughout the process of language acquisition. The development of effective strategies for assessing ELLs is a significant educational consideration, yet it is a topic of limited research. Furthermore, there is a deficit of widely shared knowledge regarding best practices in assessing ELLs, as well as a lack of researched-backed, practical, and affordable resources for assessment.

It is vital that past and current practices in assessing ELLs are considered and adjusted to ensure that quality, effective assessments are available at all stages of the ELL's development. Furthermore, assessment practices should be evaluated and revised to meet the unique and evolving sociocultural and linguistic considerations surrounding the diverse populations of English language learners.

LEGISLATION IMPACTING ASSESSMENT OF ELLS

Schools in the United States are responsible for ensuring the provision of quality education that supports academic progress while teaching English to all students, including English language learners. Currently, neither federal nor state laws specify services that must be provided to ELLs. However, there is legislation that extends some guidelines for school districts.

English language learners attending U.S. schools are protected under civil rights laws issued by the Office of Civil Rights in 1970. Under these laws, school districts are subject to violation of federal law if they fail to take "affirmative steps to rectify the language deficiency to open its instructional program to these students." It should be noted that, while districts are required to take affirmative steps, the specific actions have not been prescribed in legislation.

The Office of Civil Rights (OCR) is tasked with oversight of the school district's adherence to ensuring that ELLs are provided equal educational opportunities; however, the prescribed measures are dictated by the individual states. The No Child Left Behind Act (2001) required states to assess the progress toward English proficiency but, likewise, did not designate assessments. School districts choose which assessments to implement.

ASSESSMENT IN EDUCATIONAL SETTINGS

In the world of education, *assessment* refers to the systematic processes by which information regarding student academic progress is measured. A variety of information about students' educational progress is gathered through assessments throughout every student's educational career. Subsequently, information gathered through the assessment process is evaluated, analyzed, and documented by the professionals working with the student. The assessment information is then utilized to improve learning for all students.

How students are assessed varies greatly. Through informal classroom assessments such as teacher observation and low-stakes classroom activities to formal benchmark testing and high-stakes, state-mandated achievement tests, educators around the United States are expected to provide an ongoing assessment to every child in their classroom. Additionally, the assessment measures should be tailored to the whole class as well as match the unique needs of diverse learners. Furthermore, educators must enact ongoing tracking and analysis of the body of assessment measures implemented, and utilize results from those analyses as a driving force in selecting learning activities.

English language learners pose unique considerations when building assessment programs in schools, districts, states, and at the national level. While the universally known best practice of ongoing assessment is vital to all students, there are unique considerations that impact English language learners.

First, in any given classroom, the ELLs may represent a wide variety of languages. Secondly, they likely represent a wide variability in ability levels in their native language as well as in English. Finally, they represent unique cultural differences, known as sociocultural linguistics, that play an important role in many aspects of their learning and English language acquisition.

Language Variety

The variety of language backgrounds of students can pose challenges when attempting to comprehensively assess ELLs. While often considered in "homogenous" terms, on the contrary, ELLs represent a vast array of first languages. The unique language background of the child can be a determining factor in the progression of English proficiency (Gottlieb, 2016).

The first language spoken by a child can impact their literacy and morphological awareness (awareness of morphemic structures of words and the ability to reflect on and manipulate that structure when learning English) when learning the second language (Jiang, 2011). This reality poses a significant consideration when developing assessments because a "one-size-fits-all" assessment can be detrimental to students.

Native Language Proficiency

Research by Carroll and Bailey (2016) supports the idea that student's skills and ability in their first language have a direct impact on their ability to successfully acquire a second language. This phenomenon is due to language transfer. Positive language transfer occurs when the learner can transfer the phonology, syntax, and semantics of the native language into the learning of the second language. There are significant implications for the need for various forms of assessment that monitor the progression of language transfer since students who struggle to use their first-language literacy skills continuously struggle with literacy development in the second language.

Sociocultural Linguistics

Within the United States, English language learners are the most rapidly expanding diverse population (National Center for Education Statistics, 2021). ELL populations comprise culturally and linguistically diverse members. Classrooms are enhanced by the diversity represented by ELLs; however, the diversity within the ELL subgroup is often underestimated and/or ignored entirely in program development, including assessment planning and development (Farah, 2017).

Every learner is impacted by the social dynamics that they carry with them (Watson, 2013). This is especially true for individuals within the ELL population because not only might their sociocultural dynamics conflict with the dominant population, but they may also conflict with others classified within their subgroup (Abedi, 2011; Bailey & Kelly, 2010; Watson, 2013). Programming that ignores the sociocultural diversity of individuals will certainly come up lacking (Watson, 2013). Therefore, it is of significant consideration in assessment development to survey sociocultural factors in addition to ability-specific criteria. Specific criteria for sociocultural considerations will be explored later in this chapter.

ASSESSMENTS OF ENGLISH LANGUAGE LEARNERS

Home Language Surveys

Surveys for identifying students with limited English proficiency have been in place since the 1960s (National Center for Education Statistics, 2021). Home Language Surveys (HLS) were implemented as one of the first measures instated because of the No Child Left Behind Act of 2001. These surveys were intended to serve as an initial step in the screening process to identify a student's need for language support services. HLS surveys vary across states in the United States. However, the surveys generally pose questions about what language was first learned, language exposure, and background (Green, 2018).

While Home Language Surveys are widely utilized in U.S. education systems, how they are used may pose serious concerns that impact the validity of identifying students with limited English proficiency as well as the services provided to those students (Bailey & Kelly, 2010). Furthermore, questions regarding education equity arise from some of the practices related to HLSs (del Rosario Basterra, et al., 2011; Sireci & Faulkner-Bond, 2015). The fairness and validity of determining assessments and assessment practices are challenged by many factors.

While roughly half of the states in the United States require a HLS, all states recommend the use of some type of home language survey at the time of enrollment (National Center for Education Statistics, 2021). Title III of the No Child Left Behind Act (2001) explicitly requires that all states identify students who need language support services. Additionally, it is required that students be assessed or further screened for language proficiency within 30 days of the initial identification.

At this time, there is no mandated survey, so the types of surveys implemented vary among states. Likewise, the language services provided to students vary across states. Students qualify for language services through identification as *limited English proficient* based on the results of their school district's chosen screening process/assessment. Depending on the state, a wide or narrow net may be cast when identifying English language proficiency.

U.S. law defines *limited English proficient* as an individual "who comes from an environment where a language other than English has had a significant impact on the individual's level of English language proficiency" or who "comes from an environment where a language other than English is dominant" (NCLB Title IX, 20 U.S.C. § 9101). Students are identified as *limited English proficient* based on the results of the state's selected assessments. Once students are identified, the types of services provided to them by schools may include transitional bilingual education, dual language or bilingual maintenance programs, and structured English immersion.

Some schools may offer one or more of those services simultaneously. The voracity of support programs and services may be limited merely based on the location of the school system; there is simply no uniform, consistent system for supporting ELLs.

High-Stakes Testing

The requirements of high-stakes testing of all students in the United States have increased drastically since NCLB (2001) was enacted (Farah, 2017). There exists a complex network of proficiency and benchmark testing in each state. The interlinking of these test scores to required publication of a school "report card" grades have become a tool of dissatisfaction and limitations for countless schools. Schools are evaluated based on progress in meeting Adequate Yearly Progress (AYP) goals set forth by the states.

High-stakes assessments are utilized to judge schools and school districts on their performance, and those judgments are often driving forces in decision making. The pressure to meet AYP goals has pushed many states to imbed strenuous series of testing requirements that are imposed on all learners. Likewise, data from high-stakes assessment performance of groups of students, as well as individuals, are used in determining vital services such as program elections, student placement, and other support services.

For example, the performance of subgroups of students such as ELLs may dictate funding for programs uniquely designed to support such students in a low-performing school. Further, individual student performance is often used as a consideration when developing goals for accommodations and/or modifications for the student.

Proficiency tests, which vary across states, are intended as measures of academic progress over a given school year. However, according to Watson (2013), the instituted measures are often developed with little, if any, consideration of the complex considerations for ELLs, including sociocultural linguistic development. The lack of attention to such factors poses a serious threat to the validity of such assessments. State- and district-level assessments have far-reaching implications, but there is little data to suggest that there are systematic measures in place to ensure that the assessments have been developed with thorough consideration of the full range of needs of English language learners (Watson, 2013; Marion, et al., 2019).

ASSESSMENT VALIDITY

Validation of an assessment may be explained by the justification of the interpretations and uses of the test. Under this consideration, assessments designed or used for eliciting progress information regarding ELLs should be considered based on the intended evidence to be collected (Marion et al., 2019). The evaluation criteria should match the intended purpose of the assessment.

For example, a mathematics test should measure math skill abilities rather than the student's language ability. Research has shown that all students, including ELLs, perform better on assessments when syntax and vocabulary are simplified (Gottlieb, 2016; Sireci & Faulkner-Bond, 2015). It should be noted that all assessments, even those that are considered non–language dependent such as mathematics tests, rely on mental language to some extent.

The issue of cultural validity of assessments is imperative when considering the validity of the assessment of all learners, especially English language learners. Cultural validity takes into consideration the complex sociocultural factors that impact the way students learn and the way that they interpret test information. Mediating sociocultural factors include values, beliefs, cultural backgrounds, lived experiences, learning styles, socioeconomic factors, and patterns of communication (Abedi, 2011; del Rosario Basterra, 2011; Sireci & Faulkner-Bond, 2015).

Although considerations of cultural validity are commonly made in conventional assessment development, the measures taken often only brush the surface of addressing cultural validity. Most assessments are as much a test of language as they are of content skills and knowledge. While it is widely known that language and culture influence all areas of assessment, there is limited research and theory of language and culture to guide practices (Abedi, 2011; del Rosario Basterra, 2011; Sireci & Faulkner-Bond, 2015).

Students from diverse cultural backgrounds vary in their responses to test items, changes in topics and formatting of assessments, and their attitudes toward testing (Gottlieb, 2016). Furthermore, culture influences both the structural and the functional development of the brain as it develops (Ambady, 2011). Cultural influences on cognition, developmental differences, home language variety, differences in language status (bilingual or monolingual), and differences in reading and writing skills must be thoroughly considered in assessment development and analysis.

CLASSROOM PRACTICE

Achieving equitable and balanced assessments requires that the state, district, and classroom achieve an aligned and comprehensive system of assessing students. The system should be achieved through the utilization of multiple sources of evidence to guide decision-making. Likewise, the "system" of assessment should be comprised of formative, interim, and summative assessments that are developed to elicit analysis of student progress that is based on fair measures of their abilities (Marion et al., 2019).

Today's educators understand the need for solidly linking classroom assessments to instruction. However, those assessments must provide the opportunity for all learners at all ability levels to demonstrate their knowledge. Without the understanding that language and culture permeate all aspects of students' performance on the assessment, the selected assessments may not provide an accurate reflection of the students' abilities.

It is vital that classroom teachers become informed about assessment practices that can improve opportunities for diverse learners to demonstrate their knowledge and skills. This task also requires that teachers observe how students perform and respond, then redesign assessments to better elicit students' depth of understanding. Again, a "one-size-fits-all" approach will be ineffective, especially with English language learners.

Progress monitoring for ELLs should consist of a variety of opportunities for students to demonstrate their knowledge and skills. Additionally, accommodations and modifications should be made to suit the needs of individual students. Opportunities to demonstrate learning should include varied opportunities for written and oral demonstration of learning. Additionally, classroom teachers must offer flexibility in their expectations by adjusting or modifying assessments to meet the needs of unique learners.

ELL AND SPECIAL EDUCATION

English language learners and students with disabilities often display similar characteristics, such as difficulty understanding and using language, reading, writing, spelling, and math concepts (Abedi, 2014). Therefore, identifying ELLs with learning disabilities is a highly complex process. Although the Individuals with Disabilities Act of 2004 mandates that ELLs be tested in their native language when appropriate and in a nondiscriminatory manner, ELLs represent a disproportionate percentage of students with disabilities in the United States.

Assessments to identify ELLs with learning disabilities are complicated by linguistic diversity, as it may impact measurement error and assessment reliability. The two most-used assessments to identify students with learning disabilities, the IQ achievement discrepancy and Response to Intervention (RTI), may not consider the unique characteristics of ELLs (Abedi, 2014). To address these concerns, the body of research recommends accommodations for ELLs including directions in their native language, frequent breaks, broken-up testing sessions, visual supports, additional demonstration items, small groups, oral testing, computer-assisted testing, and other testing modifications (Abedi, 2014; Marion, 2019; Milliner & Barr, 2020). The body of research indicates that ELLs who have been provided testing accommodations perform better overall on assessments.

While testing accommodations may provide some assistance, the issue of linguistic diversity must be addressed in test-item development and all aspects of assessing ELLs. Current assessments need revision, and the processes of assessing ELLs for learning disabilities need serious reform (Chu & Flores, 2011; Abedi, 2014).

The question of appropriate, aligned, and quality assessment has been long debated in the United States (National Center for Education Statistics, 2021). Parents and educators alike have questioned the validity of various, ever-changing state and local assessments, and the use of assessment data to judge students, teachers, schools, and districts has been a sore spot for many. There is little room for doubt that assessment development and reform should be at the top of priority lists for states, and the far-reaching implications of assessments for ELLs must be at the forefront of consideration. U.S. classrooms are rapidly evolving in diversity, and education practices—including assessment—must evolve to match the needs of students. Likewise, efforts for research and theory development in the area of ELL assessment must take precedence.

REFERENCES

Abedi, J. (2014). English language learners with disabilities: Classification, assessment, and accommodation issues. *Journal of Applied Testing Technology*, *10*(2), 1–30.

Abedi, J. A. L. (2011). Assessing English language learners: Critical issues. In *Cultural validity in assessment* (pp. 65–87). Routledge.

Ambady, N. (2011). The mind in the world: Culture and the brain. *APS Observer*, *24*(5).

Bailey, A. L., & Kelly, K. R. (2010). The use and validity of home language surveys in state English language proficiency assessment systems: A review and issues perspective. *Evaluating the Validity of English Language Proficiency Assessment.*

Carroll, P. E., & Bailey, A. L. (2016). Do decision rules matter? A descriptive study of English language proficiency assessment classifications for English-language learners and native English speakers in fifth grade. *Language Testing, 33*(1), 23–52.

Chu, S. Y., & Flores, S. (2011). Assessment of English language learners with learning disabilities. *The Clearing House: A Journal of Educational Strategies, Issues and Ideas, 84*(6), 244–248.

del Rosario Basterra, M., Trumbull, E., & Solano-Flores, G. (2011). *Cultural validity in assessment: Addressing linguistic and cultural diversity.* Routledge.

Farah, M. (2017). *Accountability issues and high stakes standardized assessment: Practices, challenges, and impact for English language learners* (Doctoral dissertation, Rutgers University, Graduate School of Education).

Gottlieb, M. (2016). *Assessing English language learners: Bridges to educational equity: Connecting academic language proficiency to student achievement.* Corwin Press.

Green, A. (2018). Placement testing. In J. I. Liontas & M. DelliCarpini (Eds.), *The TESOL Encyclopedia of English Language Teaching* (pp. 1–6). Wiley-Blackwell.

Jiang, X. (2011). The role of first language literacy and second language proficiency in second language reading comprehension. *The Reading Matrix, 11*(2).

Marion, S., Thompson, J., Evans, C., Martineau, J., & Dadey, N. (2019). *The challenges and opportunities of balanced systems of assessment: A policy brief.* National Center for the Improvement of Educational Assessment.

Milliner, B., & Barr, B. (2020). Computer-assisted language testing and learner behavior. In M. R. Freiermuth & N. Zarrinabadi (Eds.), *Technology and the psychology of second language learners and users* (pp. 115–143). Palgrave Macmillan.

National Center for Education Statistics. (2021, May). *English language learners in public schools.* https://nces.ed.gov/programs/coe/indicator_cgf.asp

No Child Left Behind Act of 2001. 20 U.S.C. § 6319 (2008).

Sireci, S. G., & Faulkner-Bond, M. (2015). Promoting validity in the assessment of English learners. *Review of Research in Education, 39*(1), 215–252.

Watson, S. M. (2013). *English language learners: The impact of language and socio-cultural factors on learning.* https://council-for-learning-disabilities .org/english-language-learners-impact-of-language-and-socio-cultural-factors-on -learning

Chapter 5

Transforming Pre-Service Teacher Education

Culturally Responsive Teaching through Multicultural Children's Literature as a Vehicle of Social Change for English Language Learners

Sunyung Song

English language learners (ELLs) who speak a language other than English are the fastest-growing student population nationwide. According to the National Center for Education Statistics (2019), there are 5 million ELLs enrolled in U.S. K–12 schools. ELLs comprise more than 10% of the total K–12 public school enrollment. With a language barrier to participation and access in the education system, ELLs often face educational inequalities and have substantial academic achievement gaps (Mikow-Porto et al., 2004).

To work with ELLs from linguistically and culturally diverse backgrounds effectively, educational scholars have suggested that teachers should promote multicultural education that empowers teachers to transform schools into equitable learning environments in which all students can have an equal chance to succeed (Banks, 2002).

Yet many teacher education programs still face the challenge of adequately preparing pre-service teachers (PSTs), who are predominantly White, monolingual, and middle-class females, to become culturally responsive educators who can implement multicultural education and serve as change agents for ELLs.

One significant way to overcome this challenge in teacher education is through the utilization of culturally responsive teaching (CRT), which focuses on "using the cultural knowledge, prior experiences, frames of reference, and performance styles of ethnically diverse students to make learning encounters more relevant to and effective for [students]" (Gay, 2010, p. 31).

According to Ladson-Billings (1995), CRT has three tenets: academic success, cultural competence, and critical consciousness. In other words, implementing CRT means that teachers set high expectations for students and use students' cultural knowledge as assets for enhancing student learning (academic success). They also affirm students' culture and identity and build a bridge between home and school (cultural competence).

Moreover, they increase students' critical consciousness by addressing issues such as social justice and equity for social actions (critical consciousness). This tenet of CRT is particularly vital for socioemotional learning, which is a process through which students develop skills in managing emotions and relationships and making responsible decisions (Cho et al., 2019).

Experts in multicultural education frequently emphasize the significance of using CRT through multicultural children's literature that reflects readers' cultures, affirms their identities, and enhances their self-esteem and academic performance in literacy (Willis & Johnson, 2000). It enables teachers to disrupt the traditional literary canon of American schools and attain equitable school outcomes through critical literacy (Anderson & Irvine, 1993).

Despite the educational merits of multicultural literature being discussed in teacher education, PSTs still often feel unprepared to use this resource and develop meaningful CRT practices to respond to the cultural diversity of ELLs in mainstream classrooms (Christ & Sharma, 2018). They are potential key agents of social change for promoting educational equity for ELLs.

Therefore, it is vital for teacher education programs to provide preparation that supports PSTs' mastery of essential knowledge and skills to use CRT through multicultural literature to meet the needs of ELLs. Attention to this transformative teacher preparation is important, particularly in the southeast, in which the enrollment of K–12 ELLs increased by 350% from 1992 to 2002 (Mikow-Porto et al., 2004), and this pattern of growth has continued over the last 8 years. This chapter discusses one attempt to implement the curriculum reform that incorporated a multicultural literature-focused CRT project into an ELL methods course in an undergraduate pre-service teacher education program at a public university in Alabama.

THE STUDY

Methodology

To enhance PSTs' ability to implement CRT, the researcher redesigned the ELL methods course to include a project called Multicultural Literature for English Language Learners (MLELL), which focused on multicultural literature-enriched activities. This study examined the implementation of the MLELL project as a tool for fostering PSTs' critical engagement with multicultural literature.

Specifically, it sought to explore the potential impact of this engagement on PSTs' awareness of cultural diversity and their pedagogical practices for CRT. The study explored the following research questions:

1. How did engagement with the MLELL project increase PSTs' awareness of cultural diversity, if at all?
2. How did engagement with the MLELL project inform PSTs' CRT-integrated lesson planning and intended teaching practices for supporting ELLs, if at all?

To address the research questions above, the self-study of teacher educators' practice (S-STEP) (Loughran, 2007) was employed as a guiding framework. This S-STEP study was conducted using a qualitative phenomenological approach, which allowed the researcher to examine common lived experienced shared by all participants during the study (Creswell, 2013).

Participants

The participants were 20 undergraduate PSTs (19 females and one male) in the ELL methods course. Among the participants, 17 PSTs were in elementary education, while three PSTs were in early childhood education.

They were seniors who were at the critical transition points in their program of study prior to the internship. With the exception of two Hispanic PSTs, all participants were White and monolingual English speakers. Most of them reported feeling ill-prepared to integrate multicultural literature into their pedagogical practices.

The Instructional Design of the MLELL Project

The MLELL project focused on two major tasks: (1) class presentations on multicultural children's literature and (2) microteaching using CRT through multicultural literature (planning and teaching language arts lessons for diverse learners). In the MLELL project, the PSTs were first introduced to the tenets and strategies of CRT through readings, class discussions, and the instructor/researcher's modeling.

Then they were divided into three groups, and each group focused on one of the three major cultural minorities (Hispanic, Asian, and Islamic/Muslim cultures) that represented a significant number of ELLs in Alabama. They learned how to examine and select high-quality multicultural literature based on the criteria by Yokota (1993).

To support the PSTs' engagement with multicultural literature, a faculty librarian was invited as a course librarian. The instructor/researcher and the librarian collaboratively built a collection of multicultural books and developed LibGuides (https://libguides.athens.edu/ELL) to guide the PSTs in selecting, evaluating, and using multicultural children's books for CRT.

For class presentations, the PSTs selected more than two multicultural children's books that represented their assigned cultural group of ELLs. The presentations included (1) a book analysis of the characters, settings, and plots; (2) cultural, social, and historical information related to the literature they selected; and (3) pedagogical strategies for integrating such literature into instruction to promote CRT.

After the class presentations, the PSTs designed language arts lesson plans and integrated CRT through one of the multicultural books used for their presentation. Then, they conducted microteaching in which they ran short practice teaching sessions, video-recorded them, and exchanged peer feedback. After the completion of each task of the project, the PSTs wrote reflection journal entries.

DATA COLLECTION AND ANALYSIS

The study utilized the following multiple data sources: (1) artifacts from the project (i.e., class PowerPoint presentations, language arts lesson plans, and microteaching videos); (2) the PSTs' reflection journal entries; and (3) the researcher's field notes. The multiple data sources above were coded using a constant comparative approach, employing coding techniques borrowed from grounded theory (Creswell, 2013). Open coding, axial coding, and selective coding were used to identify salient and recurring categories in the data. Then, categories were collapsed into themes, such as growth in cultural competence and the use of multicultural literature in microteaching.

FINDINGS

Research Question 1: Increased Awareness of Cultural Diversity for Supporting ELLs

The PSTs' reflection journal entries revealed the PSTs' limited knowledge and understanding of other cultures before the MLELL project. However, the majority of the PSTs reported that the project provided them with increased awareness of cultural diversity in safe and supportive ways and that they felt better equipped to use multicultural literature to integrate CRT and enhance student learning.

The most remarkable benefit reported by the PSTs was that multicultural literature helped them examine their own misconceptions or biases about other cultures, enhance cultural competence, and develop empathy toward ELLs.

The following excerpt from a reflection journal by a PST captured increased cultural competence and empathy among the participants.

> After reading each book, I had to go back and research some of the cultural words to understand what they were. After completing this project, my cultural competence was strengthened. The multicultural books allowed me to understand how stereotypes are easy to assume when it comes to culture. They helped me reflect the biases I had and re-evaluate what I thought. . . . These books gave me an idea of what an ELL might feel like and be experiencing being a new student in a new country. ELLs are struggling to fit into their new life in America. I will be sure to include a variety of multicultural books in my future classroom library and make them feel pride in their cultural backgrounds and learn better.

As shown in the excerpt above, many PSTs articulated their understanding of the lives of ELLs that were reflected in the multilingual texts and expressed their commitment to using multicultural literature as a foundation for actively advocating for ELLs.

Research Question 2: The Impact of the MLELL Project on the PSTs' CRT-Integrated Lesson Planning and Instruction in Language Arts for Enhancing ELLs' Learning

A rubric developed by Leonard and colleagues (2014) was adapted to examine the PSTs' ability to incorporate three tenets of CRT (Ladson-Billings, 1995) through multicultural literature into language arts lessons for enhancing ELLs' learning. The PST's language art lessons (microteaching lessons with lesson plans) were rated as *substantial, cursory, superficial,* or *no evidence*. Table 5.1 shows the PSTs' text selections, learning objectives, and CRT strategies.

Table 5.1. Pre-Service Teachers' Multicultural Text Selections, Learning Objectives, and CRT Strategies

Grade Level	Examples of Multicultural Books Chosen	Examples of Learning Objectives	Examples of CRT Strategies
K	• *Happy in Our Skin* by Fran Manushkin and Lauren Tobia (2018) • *Quinito, Day and Night* by Ina Cumpiano and Jose Ramirez (2008) • *Round Is a Mooncake* by Roseanne Thong and Grace Lin (2014)	• Learn new vocabulary, using social rules of language • Identify characters, settings, and major events in a story • Analyze key words in the story to uncover the meaning of vocabulary words	• Using ELLs' first languages • Addressing the issues of kindness and peace • Discussing racial diversity • Integrating holidays, traditional foods, and daily family activities
1	• *Mei-Mei Loves the Morning* by Margaret Holloway Tsubakiyama et al. (1999) • *Abuela* by Arthur Dorros (1997) • *Golden Domes and Silver Lanterns* by Hena Khan (2012)	• Use illustrations and details in a story to describe its characters, settings, or events • Retell stories, including key details • Compare and contrast different elements of a story	• Using ELLs' cultural knowledge and prior knowledge • Discussing family traditions, travels, and daily activities • Addressing the topic of tolerance
2	• *Lon Po Po* by Ed Young (1996) • *Deep in the Sahara* by Kelly Cunnane (2018) • *The Name Jar* by Yangsook Choi (2003) • *Lucia the Luchadora* by Cynthia Leonor Garza and Alyssa Bermudez (2017)	• Ask and answer such questions as who, what, where, when, and why • Recount or describe key ideas or details from a text • Compare and contrast key details	• Using ELLs' cultural knowledge and prior knowledge • Highlighting cultural artifacts • Discussing historical figures and gender equity

3	• *Lailah's Lunchbox: A Ramadan story* by Reem Faruqi (2015) • *Maya's Blanket* by Monica Brown (2015) • *Dear Primo: A Letter to My Cousin* by Duncan Tonatiuh (2010)	• Recall information from the story and use it to write a letter to the teacher • Demonstrate understanding of the text • Ask and answer questions to monitor comprehension	• Using ELLs' first languages • Addressing religious diversity and cultural differences • Including cultural scenarios for problem solving
4	• *Grandfather's Journey* by Allen Say (1993) • *Richshaw Girl* by Mitali Perkins (2007)	• Sequence events and retell stories • Write opinion pieces, supporting a point of view with reasons and information • Make inferences from a text	• Integrating family histories and traditions • Discussing immigration and historical events • Addressing gender equity

The majority of the PSTs expressed great success in promoting the CRT tenet of academic success. This finding was confirmed when 90% of the PSTs' lessons ($n = 18$) were rated substantial. Their lessons included various CRT strategies, such as using students' cultural knowledge and first languages to facilitate the teaching-learning process. Only two PSTs' lessons were rated cursory or superficial; they passively included isolated cultural elements (e.g., holidays and foods) instead of encouraging a deeper understanding of cultural diversity.

Regarding the CRT tenet of affirming students' cultural competence, most PSTs reported being able to relate the multicultural text to ELLs' home lives or communities by addressing family histories, traditions, family travels, or daily activities. This is aligned with the analysis showing that 15 PSTs' lessons were rated substantial. For example, two PSTs' lessons focused on families' daily activities and priorities as learning contexts with reference to how they related to ELLs' home or school lives. The lessons by five PSTs were rated cursory or superficial.

As reflected in the PSTs' reflection journals, facilitating critical consciousness seemed to be the most challenging tenet of CRT. Only seven PSTs (35%) were able to explicitly connect the multicultural text to social justice or equity using class discussions or interactive activities. For instance, one PST used a multicultural text to provide a context for increasing students' awareness of religious diversity and tolerance.

Her lesson for grade 3 focused on helping students recognize and defy stereotypes about religion and included an activity to take actions for religious diversity and respect. However, the analysis revealed that nearly two-thirds of the PSTs ($n = 13$) made a cursory or superficial attempt to link the multicultural text to critical consciousness. Many of them failed to go beyond simply highlighting historical or social events to raise students' interests in the lesson. The PSTs attributed this difficulty to the fact that their lack of prior experience with context-specific issues of social justice and equity did not enable them to effectively use multicultural literature for fostering critical consciousness.

DISCUSSION AND IMPLICATIONS
FOR TEACHER EDUCATION

Although the present study represented a small group of participants within the context of one ELL methods course, it provided valuable information about the pedagogical potential of the MLELL project for empowering PSTs to utilize CRT through multicultural literature as a vehicle of social change for fostering educational equity and cultural diversity for ELLs.

Unlike previous studies (Leonard et al., 2014; Thomas & Vanderharr, 2008) in which some elementary PSTs showed resistance toward linking multicultural literature and education to teaching content knowledge, the PSTs in this study showed positive attitudes toward learning about multicultural literature and reported personal growth in cultural diversity and CRT as a result of the MLELL project.

One reasonable explanation for these positive outcomes could be that the project offered a collaborative context that strengthened the PSTs' perceptions of CRT using multicultural literature and their ability to implement it through class presentations and microteaching.

In this study, the MLELL project engaged the PSTs in planning and implementing multicultural literature-focused language arts lessons aiming to integrate the three tenets of CRT. The findings revealed many successful examples of promoting two tenets of CRT: fostering academic success and affirming students' cultural competence (Ladson-Billings, 1995). The PSTs indicated that faculty-librarian collaboration supported their exploration, evaluation, and selection of multicultural literature and helped improve their CRT-related pedagogical practices.

Despite the instructor/researcher's modeling provided, however, the project did not seem to ensure the PSTs' mastery of the skills needed to facilitate critical consciousness, which is essential for supporting ELLs' socioemotional learning. This may be due to the fact that the one-semester MLELL project was not long enough to develop the PSTs' critical reflection and problem-solving skills to foster critical consciousness.

Also, the lack of experience with classroom teaching and ELL family or community engagement might hinder them from enhancing their ability to incorporate this tenet of CRT into their lessons. This finding corroborates Huang's study (2002), which reported that 70 PSTs in early childhood, elementary, and secondary education programs at a Midwestern university achieved little success in employing the "transformation" approach (e.g., facilitating the goals of combating racism and sexism for social actions) (Banks, 2002) to planning multicultural lessons.

Planning and teaching lessons grounded in all CRT tenets and multicultural literature is a process of becoming a culturally responsive teacher that requires a great deal of time and preparatory work. Thus, pre-service teacher education programs should provide long-term, comprehensive professional development on culturally responsive teaching, social justice education, and self-transformation (Ukpokodu, 2007).

REFERENCES

Anderson, G. L., & Irvine, P. (1993). Informing critical literacy with ethnography. In C. Lankshear & P. L. McLaren (Eds.), *Critical literacy: Politics, praxis, and the postmodern* (pp. 81–104). SUNY Press.

Banks, J. A. (2002). *An introduction to multicultural education.* Allyn & Bacon.

Cho, H., Wang, C., & Christ, T. (2019). Social emotional learning of refugee English language learners in early elementary grades: Teachers' perspectives. *Journal of Research in Childhood Education, 33*(1), 40–55.

Christ, T., & Sharma, S. A. (2018). Searching for mirrors: Preservice teachers' journey toward more culturally relevant pedagogy. *Reading Horizons, 57*(1), 55–73.

Creswell, J. W. (2013). *Qualitative inquiry and research design: Choosing among five approaches* (3rd ed.). SAGE.

Gay, G. (2010). *Culturally responsive teaching: Theory, research, and practice.* Teachers College Press.

Huang, H. (2002). Designing multicultural lesson plans. *Multicultural Perspectives, 4*(4), 17–23.

Ladson-Billings, G. (1995). But that's just good teaching! The case for culturally relevant pedagogy. *Theory Into Practice, 43*, 159–165.

Leonard, J., Moore, C. M., & Brooks, W. (2014). Multicultural children's literature as a context for teaching mathematics for cultural relevance in urban schools. *The Urban Review, 46*(3), 325–348.

Loughran. J. (2007) Researching teacher education practices: Responding to the challenges, demands, and expectations of self-study. *Journal of Teacher Education, 58*(1), 12–20.

Mikow-Porto, V., Humphreies, C., Egelson, P., O'Connel, D., Teague, J., & Him, L. (2004). *English language learners in the southeast: Research, policy, and practice.* University of North Carolina Press.

National Center for Education Statistics. (2019). *English language learners in public schools.* Retrieved October 1, 2020, from https://nces.ed.gov/programs/coe/indicator_cgf.asp

Thomas, S., & Vanderharr, J. (2008). Negotiating resistance to multiculturalism in a teacher education curriculum: A case study. *The Teacher Educator, 43*(3), 173–197.

Ukpokodu, O. N. (2007). Preparing socially conscious teachers: A social justice-oriented teacher education. *Multicultural Education, 15*(1), 8–15.

Willis, A., & Johnson, J. (2000). *A horizon of possibilities: A critical framework for transforming multiethnic literature instruction.* Retrieved October 1, 2020, from http://www.readingonline.org/articles/willis/index.html

Yokota, J. (1993). Issues in selecting multicultural literature for children and adolescents. *Language Arts, 70*(3), 156–167.

Chapter 6

Recognizing Embodied Histories and Intersectionality of Students of Color in Language Teaching

Brianna R. Ramirez and Ruby Osoria

This chapter unpacks how language teaching is rooted in social, historical, and contemporary constructions of language. Teachers and practitioners are actors that can reinforce norms about language, evaluate student use of language, and implement language policy through curriculum and pedagogy. In this chapter, we draw on racist nativism (Pérez Huber et al., 2008) to discuss the politics of language underlined by colonization and white dominant histories in the United States that are present and reproduced when engaging in language teaching.

Students' linguistic assets reflect these histories, the experiences of their family and community, and their embodied intersectionalities within U.S. society and schooling. We describe the centrality of racist nativism as a lens through which we discuss how language has historically been weaponized against Communities of Color,[1] provide examples of how Students of Color experience this racist nativist history of language in current schooling, and move toward an understanding of how students experience language teaching as embodied history and intersectional identities.

At the end of the chapter, we offer guiding questions to support practitioners in critical reflection about their pedagogy with students having diverse language assets and backgrounds with the intent to justly serve students within a racially, culturally, and generationally centered approach.

In this paper, we draw on racist nativism as the guiding theoretical framework to analyze students' experiences within the context of language policies and language discourse. *Racist nativism* is defined as the assigning of values to real or imagined differences, in order to justify the superiority of the native, who is to be perceived as white, over that of the non-native, who is perceived to be people and immigrants of color, and thereby defend the rights of whites, or the natives, to dominance. (Pérez Huber et al., 2008, p. 41)

As a conceptual framework within Latina/o Critical Race Theory (LatCrit; Solórzano & Yosso, 2001), racist nativism provides the tools to recognize the racialized practices and the reinforcement of dominant hegemony that have historically affected People of Color in the United States.

As it relates to language, racist nativism is a conceptual tool that helps recognize the power structures embedded in the U.S. education system that upholds and reproduces white dominance through the english[2] language (Pérez Huber, 2011). In acknowledging the connection between language and identity, a racist nativism framework recognizes language as a tool to affirm knowledge and ways of knowing. In the context of the education system, European cultural practices and the english language are reinforced and upheld as the standard (Nieto, 1992).

Further, racist nativism recognizes the institutional impact of english-language dominance in the education system. The institutionalization of english dominance results in everyday oppression in the classroom against Students of Color through curriculum, school practices, classroom pedagogy, and educational policies (Pérez Huber, 2011).

LANGUAGE HAS HISTORICALLY BEEN WEAPONIZED AGAINST COMMUNITIES

Schooling has historically been underlined by a colonized and racist intent, with language teaching central to this mission. Such was the case with the boarding schools in the United States designed to assimilate Indigenous children into the "American" norm, which inherently meant the erasure of Indigenous culture, traditions, and language and the reproduction and domination of whiteness (Lomawaima, 1999).

Additionally, Angela Valenzuela theorized about schools as sites of "subtractive schooling" that contribute to delegitimizing and criminalizing Mexican students' cultures and language (Valenzuela, 1999). Subtractive schooling is a framework now included in *The TESOL Encyclopedia of English Language Teaching* that contributes to understanding the historical erasure of language and culture through colonization and racism in schools (Valenzuela & Rubio, 2018).

The colonial and racist history of language is upheld in current language teaching in the United States. This is evident in the continual upholding of english as the ideal, superior, or necessary language that students must learn in U.S. schools (Motha, 2006). The challenges experienced by students who are emergent english users in schools compared to students who are considered to have mastery of english indicates that schooling in the United States is structured through different underlying systems of marginality, including english dominance.

This inequity means schooling is structured to prioritize the english language, questionably, over diverse subjects' learning and success. The dominance of the english language forces a monolingual model of language identity that functions to erase the multilingualism and rich cultural histories that students bring with them to schools (Valenzuela & Rubio, 2018).

The english language has historically been utilized as a weapon of difference that dichotomously situates those considered to have mastery of the english language as superior, and othering emergent english users and learners as deficient, inferior, and ultimately "uneducated" within U.S. schooling standards (Motha, 2006). This hierarchy is a function of the english language as a tool for the promotion of white, American norms that situate the language of those who are perceived to be superior or entitled to shaping the U.S. identity as superior and educated.

This has been the colonial and racist functioning of language throughout U.S. history (Lomawaima, 1999). Therefore, the othering through language in the United States is mainly experienced by People of Color and Immigrants of Color (Motha, 2006), who hold diverse language repertoires and unique, culturally rooted ways of communicating. Understanding this history, its continued legacy in contemporary language teaching is necessary to engage in language teaching that aims to carve away at the colonial and racist histories and the harm they continue to cause for Students of Color.

STUDENTS EXPERIENCE LANGUAGE AS EMBODIED HISTORY AND INTERSECTIONALITY

Students of Color and immigrant students' experiences are directly shaped by the reproduction and upholding of dominant hegemony embedded in english-language dominance throughout their educational trajectory. Students are directly impacted by the racist nativist history embedded in their everyday schooling experience in the form of policy and the category and labeling of language.

In this context, policies and labeling are the tools used to deny opportunities and further racialize Students of Color in the classroom and beyond

(Johnson & Martinez, 1999). This is evident in the implementation of policies such as California's proposition 227 and the labeling of students as english language learners. The use of language in labeling matters, as it invokes power and colonized, racial, and linguistic history.

In 1998, California voters passed proposition 227, also known as "English for the Children." Scholars argue that proposition 227 was a response to the Latinx population growth in the 1980s and 1990s and intended to discriminate against Immigrant Communities of Color (Johnson & Martinez, 1999). Proposition 227 enforced English-only instructions across the state's public schools (Pérez Huber, 2011).

An initial impact of the implementation of the policy on Latinx students consisted of added pressure and stress. The inability to both communicate with teachers in the student's primary language and understand english-only class material resulted in students crying in class, or responding in class in a way that was labeled as a "behavior problem." For some students, proposition 227 resulted in an increase in student disengagement (Schirling et al., 2000).

Effectively, the student's primary language, Spanish, was positioned as subordinate, and the preceding outcomes resulted in the "othering" of Latinx students, having a real impact on their school experience. When reflecting on their K–12 experiences, students reported feeling alienated due to their perceived inability to communicate with their teachers in english, lack of support at school, and feeling stigmatized due to being Spanish speakers (Pérez Huber, 2011).

Students reflected on the perceived inability to communicate in english that resulted in being viewed through a deficit lens. Some students were assumed to have learning disabilities and reported being requested by their schools to take a hearing test or placed in speech therapy. These examples illustrate the language discourse that categorizes and labels students as language learners, evoking deficit framing that positions students as inferior.

The categorizing of students is often positioned as a tool to support cohorts or groups of students with similar "abilities" or "needs." What often happens is the tracking of students, which can result in a lasting impact throughout the educational trajectory. In the context of language, the categorizing of students is often done through an english-dominance framing. Students are labeled as language learners, and this labeling is not neutral.

The labeling of students' language capacities is shaped by teachers' perception toward students and their communities and further influences the implementation of pedagogical practices in an attempt to "transition" students to english proficiency (Kibler & Valdes, 2016), as opposed to understanding students as language users and recognizing students' language use and potential. Challenging the labeling of students can reposition how teachers engage with students and further affirm students' cultural ties, lived experiences, and ways of knowing (Kibler & Valdes, 2016).

Supporting students with diverse linguistic assets (Yosso, 2005) requires understanding student personal and generational histories and contemporary embodiments being acted on when engaging in this teaching. Teaching language and reinforcing language policy are not neutral acts. Through the theorization of linguistic terrorism, Gloria Anzaldúa (1999) argued, "If a person . . . has a low estimation of my native tongue, she also has low estimation of me. . . . So, if you want to really hurt me, talk badly about my language" (p. 81).

Anzaldúa argued that language is reflective of intersecting histories, identities, and experiences such as colonization, race, and culture. Language teachers with diverse linguistic students should be mindful and reflective of the various politics of language they invoke (Ladson-Billings, 1995).

The lack of consideration or intentional decentering of students' intersecting identities and language histories is evident in the mismatch students experience between their lived realities, cultures, and language teaching curriculum. Immigrant Latinx students have shared the insufficient knowledge that language instructors held about their experiences and lived realities, including migration hardships, family separation, and reunification due to immigration (Olivares-Orellana, 2020).

This has resulted in students feeling that teachers did not understand them, their families, or their academic and social needs within the classroom (Olivares-Orellana, 2020). Mismatches between english-language-learning curriculum and student realities are present in various ways. Even the examples in textbooks are not relevant or applicable to students' lives (Zotzmann, 2017).

Scholarship indicates that teachers may be mindful of students' identities, yet they only center a personal affirmation and growth approach in their teaching that aims to value students' diverse identities and experiences, without critically analyzing the history of language, race, and culture in the United States (Nelson, 2017).

Without a critical interrogation of how language has historically hurt immigrants, refugees, and Communities of Color in the United States, teachers may aim to affirm student identities without a clear understanding of the histories of marginalities that shape the daily lives of their students because of those diverse identities. This indicates the importance of teachers understanding the students they have in their classroom and the intersecting identities and complex life experiences resulting from historical systems of marginality students navigate.

This is critical for all teachers, yet particularly for english-language teachers, who are accountable to and responsible for supporting the learning of students with immigrant and refugee backgrounds and experiences. Language teachers must understand and critique their students' personal and cultural relationship to language and the historical use of english as a tool for colonization and racism in the United States.

This chapter explores the implications of language teaching that upholds english dominance and the history of colonization, subordination, and othering of immigrant students and Students of Color. In drawing from a racist nativist framework, we present a race- and culture-centered perspective that discusses how language has been weaponized against Communities of Color throughout history.

We present two examples of how this history continues to manifest in contemporary schooling experiences centered on language. To conclude, we offer critical reflection questions for practitioners to engage with throughout their pedagogical journeys to support students with diverse linguistic assets through a social justice intent that requires consistent reflection and consciousness.

These questions are by no means all-encompassing of the complexity of consciously engaging in language teaching, yet these questions can facilitate educators' critical reflection and accountability to students with diverse language backgrounds, histories, and experiences.

1. What are biases around language dominance?
2. What assumptions are made toward bilingual or multilingual students?
3. What is the impact of labeling students' abilities based on language in the classroom?
4. What barriers does language cause in the classroom?
5. What are students' connections to language?
6. In what ways do students use language in their daily lives?
7. In what ways can schools center students' home language and practices in the classroom and class assignments?
8. How are course materials accessible to students and their parents, based on language?

NOTES

1. Following the writing of some critical race theorists, we capitalize the terms *Communities of Color*, *Immigrants of Color*, *People of Color*, and *Students of Color* to engage in a project that moves toward empowerment and racial justice. I do not capitalize the term *white* in my writing to acknowledge and reject the standard grammatical norms and power represented in the capitalization of the term *white*.

2. In our writing, we do not capitalize the *english* language to engage in a political project that challenges the hegemonic dominance of english within U.S. and global society.

REFERENCES

Anzaldúa, G. (1999). *Borderlands = la frontera*. Aunt Lute Books.

Johnson, K. R., & Martinez, G. A. (1999). Discrimination by proxy: The case of proposition 227 and the ban on bilingual education. *UC Davis L. rev.*, *33*, 1227.

Kibler, A. K., & Valdes, G. (2016). Conceptualizing language learners: Socioinstitutional mechanisms and their consequences. *The Modern Language Journal*, *100*(S1), 96–116.

Ladson-Billings, G. (1995). Toward a theory of culturally relevant pedagogy. *American Educational Research Journal*, *32*(3), 465–491.

Lomawaima, K. T. (1999). *The unnatural history of American Indian education*. N.p.

Motha, S. (2006). Decolonizing ESOL: Negotiating linguistic power in U.S. public school classrooms. *Critical Inquiry in Language Studies*, *3*(2–3), 75–100.

Nelson, C. D. (2017). The-isms as interpretive prism: A pedagogically useful concept. In D. J. Rivers & K. Zotzmann (Eds.), *Isms in Language Education* (p. 15). De Gruyter Mouton.

Nieto, S. (1992). *Affirming diversity: The sociopolitical context of multicultural education*. Longman.

Olivares-Orellana, E. (2020). More than an English language learner: *Testimonios* of immigrant high school students. *Bilingual Research Journal*, *43*(1), 71–91.

Pérez Huber, L., (2011). Discourses of racist nativism in California public education: English dominance as racist nativist microaggressions. *Educational Studies*, *47*(4), 379–401.

Pérez Huber, L., Lopez, C. B., Malagón, M. C., Velez, V., & Solórzano, D. G. (2008). Getting beyond the "symptom," acknowledging the "disease": Theorizing racist nativism. *Contemporary Justice Review*, *11*(1), 39–51.

Schirling, E., Contreras, F., & Ayala, C. (2000). Proposition 227: Tales from the schoolhouse. *Bilingual Research Journal*, *24*(1–2), 127–140.

Solórzano, D. G., & Yosso, T. J. (2001). Critical race and LatCrit theory and method: Counter-storytelling. *International Journal of Qualitative Studies in Education*, *14*(4), 471–495.

Valenzuela, A. (1999). *Subtractive schooling: Issues of caring in education of US-Mexican youth*. State University of New York Press.

Valenzuela, A., & Rubio, B. (2018). Subtractive schooling. In J. I. Liontas & M. DelliCarpini (Eds.), *The TESOL encyclopedia of English language teaching* (pp. 1–7). Wiley Blackwell.

Yosso, T. J. (2005). Whose culture has capital? A critical race theory discussion of community cultural wealth. *Race Ethnicity and Education*, *8*(1), 69–91.

Zotzmann, K. (2017). Intersectionality from a critical realist perspective: A case study of Mexican teachers of English. In D. J. Rivers & K. Zotzmann (Eds.), *Isms in Language Education* (pp. 34–49). De Gruyter Mouton.

Chapter 7

The Future Is Multilingual

Chicanafuturism as Curriculum for English Language Learners

Jim L. Hollar and Jesslyn R. Hollar

Although the integration of multicultural literature in quality and quantity in PK–12 public schools has become widespread, the dead White male syndrome continues to constrain much of the curricular material that imagines the future. When up to one in four students in public schools is an English language learner (ELL), authors of color who assert other visions of the future can no longer be sidelined. The focus of this chapter is to both discuss why the curricular gap still exists and offer teachers a rationale and resources to fill it. Thankfully, this moment is met with an explosion in publication of speculative fiction meant for young adult readers. At the end of the chapter, a list of supplemental resources will be provided for teachers interested in exploring such material.

This paper presents a case for using multicultural speculative fiction, specifically Chicanafuturism, to teach science fiction and enhance present-day social discussions of race and racism specifically. This work is a deliberate attempt to value and build on English language learners' funds of knowledge (González et al., 2005) in language arts classrooms.

Chicanafuturism is the focal curricular integration for our purposes, but we acknowledge that not all ELLs are native Spanish speakers or from Spanish-speaking households. To that end, we also suggest resources to expand this visioning, such as with Indigenous futurisms, for practitioners wishing to provide additional speculative fiction texts to support ELLs in their classrooms.

ENGLISH LANGUAGE LEARNERS
AND THE CURRICULAR TURN

Research on the instruction of non-native English-speaking students focuses on the how (modes of instruction, techniques, methods, and practices) more than the what (the curriculum). Research explores and delineates program models for ELLs, including the benefits and drawbacks of sheltered instruction, bilingual models, and mainstream instruction with push-in and pull-out supports (Wright, 2015). Scholars have also enumerated high-leverage practices for ELLs, including the investigation of teacher-moves directed at supporting language acquisition across the domains of reading, writing, speaking, and listening (Ferlazzo & Sypnieski, 2012; Gibbons, 2015).

Strong instructional practices that support ELLs' language and literacy development include the deliberate selection of texts that connect to students' lived experiences and that are reflective of the students and the worlds they live in. When appropriate texts are selected to engage ELLs in the act of reading, these texts become an important vehicle to spur content-area learning. Additionally, engaging texts provide a great source of comprehensible input and begin to build a strong foundation for writing development.

While it is clear that text selection for ELLs is important, less work has been done to recommend specific, relevant texts to engage and support ELLs' literacy and language development. In formal schooling environments where English language learners may feel especially alienated from their peers and from learning, speculative fiction provides an avenue to engage in social discussions of the present day and invites conversations about past, present, and future.

CURRICULAR GAP

One of the primary functions of formal schooling is to prepare students for the future. This purpose gives science fiction texts a weight as one of the only curricular materials in schools to explicitly engage with the future. Science fiction is nothing if not a place for the imagination. Unfortunately, these courses too often narrow the imagination based on a traditional canon in terms of authors and themes: White, male, and a commentary on the relative merits of advanced technologies on society. In the standard canon of science fiction, White male authors create futurist realms that present their own problems: inhospitable climates, deepening class stratification, destructive technology, dwindling natural resources, and despotic governments.

In many schools, the science fiction material looks as it did when science fiction courses became more widespread in the 1970s. In these futurist spaces, White men are positioned as creators, colonizers, or saviors. White men envision the technology; White men control technology to their benefit; White men save mankind from impending catastrophe through their domination over technology. Such a curricular construction supports an assumed paradigm: it arranges the future as envisioned by White males. Thus, these spaces "alienate" writers and students of color.

When discussing the future within schools, we must include narratives of people of color to represent the full diversity of our present and past. However, although reconfigured in contemporary educational discourse, notions of a culture of poverty and deficit thinking continue to impact our schools. Such attitudes are part of the larger construction of students of color in our schools and represent anxieties about a future that includes people of color. Further, students of color often serve as convenient foils for the idealized White, middle-class students. These two groups are separated physically and figuratively through discourses of schooling.

One such area of separation involves how school personnel think students imagine their future. For instance, school employees carry preconceived notions of how students (and their families) are orientated toward learning new skills, saving for financial security, and delaying immediate pleasure for a future happiness (Valenzuela, 1999).

Behind these ways of seeing certain students as at-future-risk are many assumptions about how White society thinks about the future and how people of color will impact this future. We must question the ontological connection between present and future. How do such classifications affect those students positioned as disinterested in the future? Does *how* we ask students to "think about your future" reinscribe the racialized constructions that find students of color lacking in future orientation? Is a linear orientation of past, present, and future in and of itself a White, racialized ontology?

CHICANAFUTURSM: A RATIONALE FOR INCLUSION

Instead of asking ELL students to think about their future, which really means "think about my present as your teacher," we need to consider our collective future. We can then imagine conversations with young people that invite different considerations and demands of ourselves for today and tomorrow. Curricular materials focused on the future can help students and teachers engage in these speculations about futures together.

Speculative fiction is considered an inclusive term bringing together science fiction and fantasy, as well as quite a few other subgenres like supernatural, horror, and alternative history. Its inclusion of social commentary, however, can also transform how such literature is used within the schools. We must continue to strive toward a broader inclusiveness of "other" futurisms. This multicultural curricular expansion has a responsibility to live up to Banks's belief that multicultural education must be constructed for every student. The fade-to-white depiction of the future leaves many students looking for themselves on the page or on the screen.

In terms of turning theory into practice, then, Catherine Ramirez's (2008) development of "Chicanafuturism" is central here. Her work has been unique in its efforts to bring together different strands of futurisms. In the spring 2008 issue of *Aztlán: A Journal of Chicano Studies*, Ramirez made a cogent case for linking Afrofuturism with what she called *Chicanafuturism*. Simply, Ramirez's approach was to build a stronger speculative fiction genre through the inclusion of other writers of color.

Ramirez's Chicanafuturism has explored

> the ways that new and everyday technologies, including their detritus, transform Mexican American life and culture. It questions the promises of science, technology, and humanism for Chicanas, Chicanos, and other people of color. And like Afrofuturism, which reflects diasporic experience, Chicanafuturism articulates colonial and postcolonial histories of *indigenismo*, *mestizaje*, hegemony, and survival. (Ramirez, 2008, p. 187)

Here, she described a logical relationship between speculative fiction genres that would support their use with English language learners. Ramirez's work showed how science fiction curricula can diversify and thus better serve diverse classrooms. A central contention here is that all students, and particularly students of color, benefit from a curriculum that evokes their visions of the future.

Such classroom work can help students of color push back against a limited presentation of the future, featuring a myriad of robots and automatons, but only one variety of human being: White and monocultural. A curricular shift toward a multicultural and multilingual future counters the narrative of American exceptionalism often at the symbolic center of most of the literature students read in school.

A language of possibility offers students an agentive capacity to construct and reconstruct the/their futures. Speculative fiction gives ELLs the agency to construct both their own individual futures and societal futures by providing opportunities to talk about the present with speculative "distance" and reconfigure "the future" in various combinations.

EXAMPLE OF CURRICULAR INCLUSION

Whether monstrous or cuddly, the alien exists as a powerful trope across several cultural forms in American society. Indeed, there is perhaps nothing as simultaneously recognizable and unrecognizable as the alien in popular culture. As curricular material then, this "alien" provides a placeholder for students to contemplate the role of the immigrant in the world, and in American society specifically.

To do this, however, students must encounter a variety of ways this figure is depicted. As stated above, White male authors are too often the ones to envision the meaning of the "little green man" in our collective imagination. Authors of color, and especially those who speak as this "border-crosser," are crucial for students to engage with as they consider complex ideas like immigration. What follows here, then, is one way these authors can be presented as curricular material in order to engage all students with these concepts.

1. Show students this video clip of unexplained appearances of metal monoliths: https://www.youtube.com/watch?v=8Dsw8XBBjSA
   - As an anticipatory set, this video clip provides visual and verbal information to support comprehensible input for students prior to engaging with the text.
2. Ask students to think-pair-share: Do you think aliens exist? Could an extraterrestrial (explain to students that this means "outside of Earth") be responsible for the metal monoliths?
   - Think-pair-shares are instructional techniques used to support time to think and encourage low-stakes oral communication prior to whole-class sharing.
3. Then, read aloud the following passage excerpted from Gina Ruiz's (2013) *Chanclas & Aliens: A Choloverse Story*:

The aliens above watched from their strangely shaped ship wondering what manner of creature these tattooed, brown gods were . . . or so they seemed to the tiny and bent luminescent creatures invading their planet with destruction in mind. To their race, only gods were tall.

   - The read-aloud technique is used to ensure comprehension of complex text for English language learners. It also supports language acquisition in the listening domain. The passage should also be provided for students to access visually.
4. After reading the passage, the teacher asks students to think-pair-share their thoughts about passage, asking the following questions:
   a. What do you think of when you hear the word *alien*?

　　b. What stands out to you in this passage?
　　　　• During discussion of the passage, the teacher should model mark-
　　　　　ing up the text and responding to cues about the text as a means to
　　　　　support independent textual annotation.
　5. After this discussion, co-construct a definition of the word *alien*.
　　　　• Provide this definition visually and verbally, and ask learners to draw
　　　　　a picture that represents the definition of *alien*. Using multiple modes
　　　　　to represent information supports language learning.
　6. Present learners with the term *nativism*, which—while containing a
　　　negative connotation with respect to policies of favoring native inhabit-
　　　ants—also supports the revival or perpetuation of indigenous cultures.
　　　　a. Definition of *nativism*: "(n) a policy of favoring native inhabit-
　　　　　ants as opposed to immigrants, or the revival or perpetuation of
　　　　　an indigenous culture especially in opposition to acculturation"
　　　　　(Merriam-Webster, n.d.)
　　　　b. Ask students to brainstorm some ways to revise and/or privilege
　　　　　their cultures in the classroom and in their future spaces (i.e., work-
　　　　　places, institutions of higher learning, businesses, etc.).
　7. Read Gina Ruiz's *Chanclas & Aliens: A Choloverse Story.*

The central goal with the above activity is to showcase the variety of curricular forms these ideas can take within the classroom space. However, the
centering of the voice of Ruiz is intentional and must be considered essential
to this work.

This chapter has made a case for why it is necessary to include Chicanafuturism
and speculative fiction by authors of color in classrooms. The next step will
be to build a curricular repository offering examples and annotated commentary with suggestions for how to use speculative fiction to engage learners in
conversations about re-visioning the/their futures.

As institutions, schools too often construct futures for English language
learners, ascribing to them notions of success and failure based on language
"ability" rather than empowering their own self-construction. To work against
this, we encourage teachers to question how words like *past, present,* and
future are used within schooling. Teachers should question how schools
encourage certain students to become "future-oriented" while other students
are not similarly acted on. And perhaps, most importantly, teachers should
interrogate who benefits from this particular visioning, who (by contrast)
does not, and to what end? Such an orientation serves as a gatekeeper to
opportunity.

All students, but particularly students of color, benefit from a curriculum
that invites their own visions of the future. Such classroom work can help

students of color push back against the limited futures presented to them. A curricular shift toward a language of possibility counters the metanarrative of American exceptionalism often at the symbolic center of much of the literature students read in school. However, Chicanafuturism can help students resist the "alienation" of mainstream culture and envision a future of their own making. ELL students must be allowed to construct the future as well as their place in it.

SUPPLEMENTAL RESOURCES FOR CURRICULAR INCLUSION

Anthologies

- *Speculative Fiction for Dreamers*, edited by Alex Hernandez, Matthew David Goodwin, and Sarah Rafael Garcia (2021)
- *Latinx Rising: An Anthology of Latinx Science Fiction and Fantasy*, edited by Matthew David Goodwin (2020)
- *Walking the Clouds: An Anthology of Indigenous Science Fiction*, edited by Grace L. Dillon (2012)
- *So Long Been Dreaming: Postcolonial Science Fiction & Fantasy*, edited by Nalo Hopkinson and Uppinder Mehan (2004)

Websites

- Oxford Bibliographies: Latino Science Fiction: https://www.oxfordbibliographies.com/view/document/obo-9780199913701/obo-9780199913701-0112.xml#obo-9780199913701-0112-bibItem-0001
- La Bloga's Latino Speculative Literature Directory: https://labloga.blogspot.com/2014/01/la-blogas-latino-speculative-literature.html

Sampling of Novels and Short Story Collections

- *Roachkiller and Other Stories*, by Richie Narvaez (a short story collection; 1992)
- *Infinity Ring: Curse of the Ancients*, by Matt de la Peña (2013)
- *Summer of the Mariposas*, by Guadalupe Garcia McCall (2012)
- *The Closet of Discarded Dreams*, by Rudy Ch. Garcia (2012)

REFERENCES

Ferlazzo, L., & Sypnieski, K. H. (2012). *The ESL/ELL teacher's survival guide: Ready-to-use strategies, tools, and activities for teaching all levels.* Wiley.

Gibbons, P. (2015). *Scaffolding language, scaffolding learning: Teaching English language learners in the mainstream classroom.* Heinemann.

Global News. (2020, December 7). *Wild theories spread about mysterious monoliths appearing across the globe* [Video]. YouTube. https://www.youtube.com/watch?v=8Dsw8XBBjSA

González, N., Moll, L. C., & Amanti, C. (2005). *Funds of knowledge: Theorizing practices in households, communities, and classrooms.* Routledge.

Merriam-Webster. (n.d.). Nativism. Retrieved September 29, 2021, from https://www.merriam-webster.com/dictionary/nativism

Ramirez, C. (2008). Afrofuturism/Chicanfuturism: Fictive kin. *Aztlán: A Journal of Chicano Studies, 33*(1), 185–194.

Ruiz, G. (2013, September 3). *Chanclas & aliens.* https://www.ginaruiz.com/stories/chanclas-and-aliens

Valenzuela, A. (1999). *Subtractive schooling: Issues of caring in education of US-Mexican youth.* State University of New York Press.

Wright, W. (2015). *Foundations for teaching English language learners: Research, theory, policy, and practice.* Caslon Publishing.

Chapter 8

A Critical Multicultural Analysis of English Learners in Picturebooks

Amina Chaudhri

Slowly, like clouds lifting, things became clearer. Sticks and chicken feet became letters. Sputters and coughs became words. And the words had meanings. Every day Mari understood more and more. (Aliki, 1998, n.p.)

The epigraph above captures the impression of young Mari, the protagonist of *Marianthe's Story: Painted Words* (Aliki, 1998), as the English language became gradually more accessible to her. The text is accompanied by two images: one of Mari studying her books by lamplight, her expression serious with determination; the second of Mari and her friend smiling together in a playground. This scene could be interpreted as representative of the experience of many young English learners (ELs), for whom acquiring new language skills is colored with both anxiety and hope.

According to a Pew Research report (Bialik et al., 2018), in 2015 there were nearly 5 million ELs in public schools in the United States, with all indications that the number is steadily rising. For educators, this means ensuring that their classroom environments and curricula are appropriate and inclusive. Progressive models of curriculum recognize that the potential for social transformation lies in the methods and materials that educators use with their students. In a political climate that is openly hostile to people who do not speak English, supporting multilingualism is an act of resistance that seeks to undermine limited, hegemonic, English-only perspectives.

One way that educators can counter negative discourse is to include children's literature that affirms and validates the experiences of ELs through story and art. An abundance of research supports critical uses of children's and young adult literature that provides readers with the windows and mirrors that reflect the diversity of their worlds (Fleming et al., 2015).

Picturebooks that depict characters who are multilingual or in the process of learning English can be instrumental in developing students' awareness of language acquisition. Well-written stories with interesting plots, developed characters, and appealing illustrations can affirm life experiences of readers who find points of connection. They can inspire empathy, provide humor, and provoke indignation. They can also invite critique. All these responses should be encouraged as part of the "transaction" of reading (Rosenblatt, 1978).

Studies in literacy, ESL, and TESOL have demonstrated that children's books that depict ELs in a positive light can have a favorable impact on young readers and learners of English (Cummins et al., 2005; Moses and Kelly, 2017; Serafini, 2004). In their examination of literacy narratives, Botelho and Rudman (2009) provided analyses of children's books representing ELs, arguing that a critical multicultural analysis of such texts provides transformative pedagogical opportunities to educators and students. This chapter builds on that research.

CRITICAL MULTICULTURAL ANALYSIS

Critical multicultural analysis (CMA) is both a theoretical lens and a methodology. As a theoretical lens, a core tenet is the assumption that all texts are imbued with the historical, social, and political ideologies of the contexts in which they are created. In other words, texts are not neutral. As a methodology, CMA provides the tools that enable readers (both adult and child) to make those ideologies visible.

With regard specifically to literacy, CMA recognizes that literacy involves more than skills-based language acquisition and is dependent on context: "Literacy processes are not just cognitive processes or a set of skills stored in people's heads. Literacies are social practices, connected to and constructed by everyday practices and many contexts" (Botelho & Rudman 2009, p. 42).

Picturebooks that echo culturally responsive patterns of practice add depth and meaning in a format that is accessible to early elementary grade readers. The selection of picturebooks analyzed here is curated using a CMA lens to make visible the explicit and implicit ideologies embedded in picturebooks depicting ELs and the process of language acquisition; to describe the degree to which language acquisition is depicted as a social practice; and to suggest pedagogical possibilities for which these books are suited.

LANGUAGE ACQUISITION AS A SOCIAL PRACTICE

Botelho and Rudman (2009) advocated engaging children with narratives that move beyond the mainstream modalities of literacy (skill-based reading and writing), in favor of texts that value children's lives outside of school (p. 46). A tenet of CMA is that literacy of all types must be grounded in the learner's life experience, crossing between school, home, and community realms.

To the extent that the brevity of the format of the picturebook allows, all the books in this corpus depict the acquisition of language as fully integrated in the ELs' social practices, be it through friendships with peers or connections with adults, spanning school, home, and community contexts. Additionally, some books feature ELs who share their heritage language with English speakers, suggesting an appreciation of multilingualism.

English Learners in the Context of School

School is a formative learning context for children in general, and for ELs in particular, the experience is often one of cultural as well as linguistic negotiation. The children featured in these picturebooks are recent immigrants to the United States, and the books open with their first few days of school. Readers must interact with text and images that depict varying degrees of anxiety that the EL characters feel.

Teachers can guide students to discuss these experiences, making connections between the texts and themselves and their peers. ELs who share the characters' experiences may feel validated by the fact that stories similar to their own can be found in books. ELs who are comfortable and confident might volunteer to share their levels of connection, but must not be put on the spot to do so.

Hee Jun in *A Piece of Home* (Watts & Yum, 2016) felt "ordinary" at home in Korea, but physically and linguistically "different" in West Virginia (n.p.). The illustrations depict him as the only Asian in the class, and although his classmates appear friendly and approachable, he is scowling and withdrawn. Hee Jun describes the sound of English as a "sharp noise" and English names "like stones on my tongue" (n.p.). It is made explicit that language is the main barrier between Hee Jun and his new world. A well-intentioned teacher tries to help, making the mistake of speaking slowly, "as if I am stupid" (n.p.). But if her efforts are clumsy, Hee Jun's reluctance to try doesn't help. He does not want to be there and puts his head down on his desk to signal as much.

A similar level of discomfort is evident in body language and facial expressions of Carmen in *Carmen Learns English* (Cox & Dominguez, 2010), Saoussan in *From Far Away* (Munsch et al., 2017*),* Blanca in *No English*

(Jules & Huntington, 2007), Juanito in *The Upside Down Boy* (Herrera & Gómez, 2000), Mari in *Marianthe's Story* (Aliki, 1998), and Ana in *Home at Last* (Elya & Davalos, 2002). Visually, the downcast eyes and slumped shoulders of these characters communicate vulnerability. Teachers might invite students to consider these visual cues as a way of recognizing and understanding nonverbal language. ELs themselves might find affirmation in the textual and visual recognition of their own experiences. These are likable, sympathetic characters depicted in appealing artistic styles so that they draw the readers' attention even before plots and personalities are developed.

Ovando and colleagues (2006) reminded us that educators have a responsibility for providing an environment that supports ELs both linguistically and culturally. Several picturebooks address this concept in a variety of ways through the actions of classroom teachers. Ana's teacher welcomes Ana into the class and encourages all the students to help her practice phrases in English. Blanca's teacher asks all the students for ideas to make Blanca feel welcome, and they suggest learning about Argentina and greeting her in Spanish. Further, the principal displays Blanca and Diane's drawings under a banner titled "Making New Friends" that elicits compliments from the wider school community.

Juanito's teacher, Mrs. Sampson, recognizes his fine singing voice and teaches him a song in English for him to sing before an audience. This boosts his confidence and sets him on an upward learning trajectory. Saoussan's teacher hugs her "like my mother" (n.p.) when she is afraid, and Carmen's teacher picks up on Carmen's Spanish speech to teach the whole class the English and Spanish equivalents of greetings, numbers, and other common phrases.

Some teachers are less active and more patient in their approaches, allowing ELs to take their time, prepared to step in when the children signal that they are ready. Mari's teacher in *Marianthe's Story* encourages her to express herself through drawing, and a significant moment occurs when he uses a painting she made about being hurt by an unkind classmate as a teachable moment to address the class. When she is ready, Mari is asked to share her story with the class. She does so with the pictures she has drawn and with the words she has learned thus far.

Similarly, in *My Name is Yoon* (Recorvits & Swiatkowska, 2003), the teacher is patient as Yoon takes her time before she prints her name in English, communicating through jokes and smiles that she knows Yoon needs to find her own way into the community. Juana, the protagonist of *Dear Abuelo* (Dominguez & Martinez, 2019), makes a friend who encourages her to correct the teacher's mispronunciation of her name. Text and image describe the teacher as happy to have learned of her error. In *One Green Apple*

(Bunting & Lewin, 2006), Farah's teacher smiles at her to communicate that adding her green apple to the group's red apples is okay.

The teachers in the books above are depicted as making a concerted effort to welcome the new EL students into the classroom, and to varying degrees, they draw on their strengths to help them establish themselves as members of the group. As such, they represent constructivist teaching practices that make room for the entirety of children's lives and value their funds of knowledge (Moll & Amanti 2005). Young readers who are guided to observe the behavior of the adult characters in the books will develop a nuanced understanding of the dynamics between children and adults, teachers and students.

The EL characters in these books are initially, understandably reticent or resistant to their new school environments. They read facial expressions, gestures, and body language to gain a sense of their classmates—also accessible to readers through the illustrations. Some authors and illustrators include secondary characters who tease or express hostility toward the EL characters. For example, Farah notices the cold looks and unfriendly tones of some of her classmates. When Carmen starts to speak in English, some boys tease her about her accent, and a boy in Mari's class calls her names. Juana's teacher mispronounces her name. These are realistic elements that are all too familiar for ELs, and their inclusion in the books will affirm their experiences and hold up mirrors for readers who harbor the same feelings as the bullies.

Once they have gained confidence, Farah, Carmen, Mari, and Juana stand up for themselves, correcting any perceptions that they are to be teased or pitied. These EL characters are portrayed as children with agency, especially when supported by friends. In this way, these picturebooks counter the perception of ELs as passive or easily victimized.

HOME AND COMMUNITY: LEARNING THROUGH KINSHIP

Language acquisition is meaningful and lasting when it is part of a social process such as making friends, or within a relevant context. This process is evident in many of the picturebooks in which friendships between children are opportunities for sharing language and culture. Although the acquisition of English is presented as necessary to the successful integration of the EL child or adult into their new community, the authors and illustrators of the books described in this section are careful to balance this need with an appreciation of heritage languages. Thus, while English-speaking friends teach their EL peers, the reverse is also true.

In *Dear Abuelo* (Dominguez & Martinez, 2019), Juana's first day at school is spoiled when, in addition to feeling alone, her teacher mispronounces her name, making her feel even more different. At home, she learns that she was named for her grandmother, which makes her proud and determined to keep learning English. Soon she makes a friend who is also from Mexico and is bilingual. In her letters to Abuelo, Juana describes her progress in becoming bilingual with her new friend. Illustrations depict the happy girls drawing and labeling pictures of each other. In the context of learning about her connection to her grandmother, and the possibility of being bilingual like Elizabeth, Juana is motivated and confident.

Despite his initial resistance, Hee Jun learns to "form words to make their meaning clear" (n.p.). His learning is not depicted, and the implication is that he stopped resisting and opened up to his new life. Dialogue bubbles of Hee Jun speaking English with his friend Steve and teaching him words in Korean suggests that his progress is happening in this social realm. Furthermore, Hee Jun's grandmother has made friends with Se Ra's teacher who helps her with English and, in return, gets advice about life. Thus, both characters' adjustment to life in the United States, in English, is mitigated through friendships and reciprocity.

Three books take a different approach to the idea of the sharing of language grounded in cultural experiences and intergenerational relationships. In *Mango, Abuela, and Me* (Medina & Dominguez, 2015), *Grandfather Counts* (Cheng & Zhang, 2000), and *Uncle Rain Cloud* (Johnston & VandenBroeck, 2001), the ELs are adult immigrants who negotiate their new lives through children with whom they develop reciprocal relationships. In *Mango, Abuela, and Me*, Abuela leaves her home country to live with her family in the United States.

She and Mia share a room, and they spend a lot of time together: Not knowing each other's language is a barrier that makes them sad. One day, Abuela teaches Mia how to make empanadas, and they name the ingredients for each other in Spanish and English. Next, they begin to play *Oye y Di*—"Hear and Say," labeling objects around the house with their name cards, similar to the practice in many classrooms. The illustrations suggest that the focus is on Abuela learning English, while the implication is that Mia is simultaneously learning Spanish. This slight imbalance suggests a subtle privileging of English over Spanish.

As their communication develops, Abuela shares stories about Abuelo and their home. Illustrations depict Abuela and Mia looking visibly happy while they share their stories: "Best of all, now when Abuela and I are lying next to each other in our beds, our mouths are full of things to say" (n.p.).

This motif is echoed in *Grandfather Counts*, in which Helen and her Gong Gong, recently arrived from China, begin to cross the language barrier between them by counting the train cars that rush by their window. Gong Gong counts in Chinese, teaching Helen, and she responds in English, teaching him. Later, at the dinner table, Gong Gong tells the children about their ancestral name, and there is a suggestion of the children learning Chinese with his support.

Uncle Rain Cloud provides a different expression of the powerlessness a person can feel when they are linguistically isolated. Having recently moved from Mexico to the United States, Carlos's Tío Tomás is clearly angry at having to negotiate a world in English. He scowls and declares that English words sound ugly.

His resistance can be understood as a manifestation of the difficulty he experiences as he adjusts. In complete contrast, Tío Tomás's disposition changes when he is at home. He tells Carlos stories about Mexico, tales about "tongue-twister gods" with names in Nahuatl that Carlos loves to learn to say faster and faster, stumbling and laughing over their pronunciations. Tío reveals his helplessness to Carlos: "I feel like a broken-winged bird. A thing that just flops around. You speak for me, a grown man, because . . . I am afraid to speak English" (n.p.).

Like Carlos, young readers might be surprised at this adult's admission of helplessness, prompting empathy. He assures his uncle that he has felt the same way, and that he has learned to ignore people who tease him. After this breakthrough, Tío Tomás makes an effort, and Carlos helps him read and pronounce words. Their relationship is clearly one of trust and mutual respect as Tomás continues to teach Carlos in Spanish about his heritage.

These books contain a powerful message about one of the many elements of the immigrant experience: adjusting to a world in a different language. Juxtaposed with books in which children are the ELs, these books are credible in their depiction of the adjustment being harder for adults than it is for children. What they have in common is that language is just one of many factors in the development of relationships with friends and community, and that the absence of English is paired with a proficiency in a heritage language that can be shared within those relationships.

All these books depict the presence of the EL as an asset to the family, bringing with them a cultural connection that had been lost with time and distance. Authors and illustrators are tender in their renditions of these older immigrants' experiences. The first-person narrators posit readers in alignment with the children from whose perspectives readers witness the isolation and sadness that the adults experience at being in an unfamiliar context with limited linguistic access

Furthermore, these stories present a balanced view of language acquisition: there is a symbiotic connection between the grandparents who only speak their heritage language and the grandchildren who only speak English. The hierarchy of an EL as deficient is disrupted in favor of the potential bilingualism of both generations.

VALUING HERITAGE LANGUAGES AND CULTURES

The importance of affirming students' heritage languages while they acquire English is well established in bilingual and ESL education. Furthermore, research and practice in culturally responsive pedagogy make clear that meaningful learning happens when learning is connected to prior knowledge, and past and current experiences.

The teacher in *Carmen Learns English* introduces herself to Carmen in Spanish. Carmen notes that she sounds "muy terrible!" (n.p.) and is comforted by the recognition that this teacher would not make fun of her English. Carmen does not understand the lyrics of a song the students learn about a yellow bus. Later that day, her teacher points out the yellow school bus, and Carmen makes the connection immediately.

In this way, the teacher continues to connect words and concepts in English within a context that makes them immediately accessible to Carmen. She invites Carmen to teach the class what she knows in Spanish. Carmen practices what she learns in English so she can teach her younger sister. Thus, Carmen's learning at school crosses easily into what she needs to do at home in order to prepare her sister for school.

In addition to adults, peers can value ELs' heritage languages as they form friendships. The narrator of *No English*, Diane, feels remorse for having embarrassed Blanca for drawing instead of writing. To make amends, she asks the librarian to find her a book in Spanish, and she and Blanca point out the words in English and Spanish respectively. They communicate through drawings that they label with names, and their friendship grows.

Blanca and Diane's efforts are celebrated at school. One illustration shows an "All About Me" poster by Blanca that includes a map of Argentina and pictures. Blanca teaches her friends jump rope rhymes in Spanish, and everyone counts in Spanish. *No English* invites readers to examine the power of friendship, the importance of understanding the consequences of unkind words, and the benefits of being multilingual.

The Day Saida Arrived (Redondo & Wimmer, 2020) takes the power of peer connections in the sharing of language to a deeper level, both textually and visually. The narrator notices that her new classmate, Saida, is silent and sad, "has lost all her words" (n.p.). The illustration is a close-up of a girl's tearful face, with letters of the Arabic alphabet seeming to float out of her head. The girls communicate with drawings, forging a connection. The narrator's mother tells her about Saida's home in Morocco, and her father explains that Saida has not lost her words; she simply cannot use the ones she has because they are different, adding, "In Morocco . . . yours wouldn't work either" (n.p.).

Thus, the potential for a linguistic hierarchy that subverts Arabic is precluded. The narrator decides to learn about Morocco, and the girls embark on a shared exchange of languages. They teach each other the words for their school materials and laugh as they stumble over unfamiliar pronunciations. They understand the power of words to hurt and heal. Both text and illustrations include words in English and Arabic, and images of culturally specific salience to the girls' friendship. *The Day Saida Arrived* is unique in this corpus of books for its lyrical text; seamless blending of language, culture, and companionship; and the balanced valuing of Arabic and English.

SUGGESTIONS FOR CLASSROOM USE

Educators who include picturebooks featuring ELs should be intentional in their purposes and practices so as not to pigeonhole the experiences, and by extension, their EL students. Ideally, classroom libraries should include all the titles discussed here so that readers have access to the diversity in form and content that these books provide, and while it is important that readers see themselves represented, it is equally important that they learn about the language-acquisition experiences of children from cultures different from their own.

These books are well suited to being read aloud to young students. Teachers can model fluency and direct students to take note of the relationship between text and image. Bilingual books serve the dual purpose of appealing to the heritage language readers, and exposing linguistic outsiders to another form of language. *The Upside Down Boy*; *Mango, Abuela, and Me*; *Uncle Rain Cloud*; *My Name Is Yoon*; *The Day Saida Arrived*; and *A Piece of Home* encourage bilingual readings.

All of these titles can be included thematically in text sets. *A Piece of Home*, *Dear Abuelo*, *The Day Saida Arrived*, and *No English* have strong themes of friendship. *Carmen Learns English*, *Marianthe's Story*, and *Home at Last* could be used in discussions about how to stand up to bullies, and *A Piece of Home*, *Grandfather Counts*, *Marianthe's Story*, *Home at Last*, and *One Green Apple* lend themselves naturally to units on immigration. Themes of family are present in almost all the books. Ultimately, with a little creativity and purpose, teachers can use this set of books in myriad ways, integrating well-developed EL characters as naturally as they would include other types of diversity.

REFERENCES

Aliki. (1998). *Marianthe's story: Painted words*. Greenwillow Books.

Bialik, K., Scheller, A., & Walker, K. (2018, October 25). *6 facts about English language learners in U.S. schools*. Pew Research Center. Retrieved November 10, 2020, from https://www.pewresearch.org/fact-tank/2018/10/25/6-facts-about -english-language-learners-in-u-s-public-schools

Botelho, M. J., & Rudman, M. K. (2009). *Critical multicultural analysis of children's literature: Mirrors, windows, and doors*. Routledge.

Bunting, E., & Lewin, T. (2006). *One green apple*. Clarion Books.

Cheng, A., & Zhang, A. (2000). *Grandfather counts*. Lee & Low Books.

Cox, J., & Dominguez, A. (2010). *Carmen learns English*. Holiday House.

Cummins, J., Bismilla, V., Chow, P., Cohen, S., Giampapa, F., Leoni, L., Sandhu, P., & Shastri, P. (2005, September). Affirming identity in multilingual classrooms. *Educational Leadership, 63*(1), 38–43.

Dominguez, G. H., & Martinez, T. (2019). *Dear Abuelo*. Reycraft Books.

Elya, S. M., & Davalos, F. (2002). *Home at last*. Lee & Low Books.

Fleming, J., Catapano, S., Thompson, C. M., & Carrillo, S. R. (2015). *More mirrors in the classroom: Using children's literature to increase literacy*. Rowman & Littlefield.

Herrera, J. F., & Gómez, E. (2000). *The upside down boy/El nino de cabeza*. Children's Book Press.

Johnston, T., & VandenBroeck, F. (2001). *Uncle rain cloud*. Talewinds.

Jules, J., & Huntington, A. (2007). *No English*. Mitten Press.

Medina, M., & Dominguez, A. (2015). *Mango, Abuela, and me*. Candlewick Press.

Moll, L. C., & Amanti, C. (2005). *Funds of knowledge: Theorizing practices in households, communities, and classrooms* (N. Gonzalez, Ed.). Routledge.

Moses, L., & Kelly, L. B. (2017). The development of positive literate identities among emerging bilingual and monolingual first graders. *Journal of Literacy Research, 49*(3), 393–423.

Munsch, R., Askar, S., & Green, R. (2017). *From far away*. Annick Press Ltd.

Ovando, C. J., Combs, M. C., & Collier, V. P. (2006). *Bilingual and ESL classrooms: Teaching in multicultural contexts* (4th ed.). McGraw-Hill.

Recorvits, H., & Swiatkowska, G. (2003). *My name is Yoon*. Frances Foster Books.

Redondo, S. G., & Wimmer, S. (2020). *The day Saida arrived*. Blue Dot Kids Press.

Rosenblatt, L. M. (1978). *The reader, the text, the poem: The transactional theory of the literary work*. Southern Illinois University Press.

Serafini, F., (2004). Images of reading and the reader. *The Reading Teacher, 57*(7), 610–617.

Watts, J., & Yum, H. (2016). *A piece of home*. Candlewick Press.

Chapter 9

Assessment of English Learners

Adopting a Cultural Validity
Assessment Framework

Eric J. López and Esther Garza

As our country continues to develop and evolve its multicultural tapestry, assessment practices and outcomes for students who are culturally and linguistically diverse become of central focus and increase the need for the development of culturally valid and relevant assessments. In this chapter, we explore how adopting a culturally valid assessment that considers environmental, contextual factors that impact learning for English learners (EL) can construct a framework that calls for including students who bring different linguistic and cultural practices for learning. ELs in this chapter are defined as students who bring a language other than English to classroom learning.

To extend and highlight this conceptualization of an EL for assessment purposes, the authors want to emphasize the significance of environmental, contextual factors that ELs bring to learning. The contextual factors include generational differences, variation in language, different language-proficiency levels, immigration (documented and undocumented status), race, ethnicity, and class. These contextual differences are conflated with the academic needs requiring programs such as special education, gifted and talented, bilingual and dual-language education, and English as a Second Language (ESL), which demand a range of assessments to support ELs' linguistic and literacy needs (Liasidou, 2013, p. 12).

The increase in the population of ELs in the United States continues to steadily rise. The increase in the EL population supports continued research in exploring efforts to ensure that assessments used to evaluate ELs supply assessment practices that reflect the strengths and challenges that ELs face in academic learning in their first (L1) and second language (L2), as over 20% of school-age students in the United States speak a language other than English in the home environment (Kritkos et al., 2018, p. 331).

The Department of Education identified ELs as the fastest-growing educational subgroup in the United States (National Research Council, 2011, p. 7). Between the years 2009–2010 and 2014–2015, there was an increase in ELs in more than half of the states, with a notable increase of 40% in five states (U.S. Department of Education, 2018). As the EL population continues to rise, it is pertinent that researchers and educators design assessment practices and instruments that provide an accurate picture of ELs' linguistic and academic needs to fulfill student learning.

The role of culture and language in the development of assessments critically impacts the performance outcomes of ELs. As early as the 1930s, there was concern for culture and language needing to be considered in the assessment of ELs (Sanchez, 1932). When language and culture are not considered but are ignored in the development and norming of an assessment, the results of the data based on student outcomes will impact the instructional decisions made for ELs.

These decisions are connected to future opportunities for self-growth, development, and personal advancement (Sattler et al., 2018). This lays the groundwork for a cultural validity assessment framework and prevents educators from making assumptions based on suboptimal characteristics (Myers et al., 2018, p. 756). Specific factors associated with cultural validity are discussed to provide an overview of considerations educators and practitioners must examine when assessing ELs.

TESTIMONIOS AS PERSONAL NARRATIVES ABOUT TESTING PRACTICES FOR ELS

To move forward and center the assessment of ELs in culturally and linguistically inclusive ways, assessment must establish a connection between language and culture when (1) planning, (2) designing, (3) constructing, (4) administering, (5) scoring, (6) norming, and (7) interpreting results of assessments for ELs. Moreover, an assessment framework must consider the importance of language and culture as equally interrelated processes of human development that, when assessed and evaluated, should inform the assessment practices and further operationalize this established connection.

As the field of assessment evolves, researchers and educators should consider the valuable use of *testimonios* to understand how to address the cultural and linguistic needs of ELs that exist in a myriad of ways as contextual factors of immigration, generational type (i.e., first, second generation), language proficiency, and socioeconomic status.

Setting the chapter authors' positionality through personal *testimonio* (Bernal et al., 2017; Fuentes & Pérez, 2016), narratives of trauma, healing, and perseverance with assessment will further set the cultural relevance and impetus behind applicable processes and tools for appropriately assessing ELs. This also lays the groundwork for the development of a critical consciousness (Valenzuela, 2016) to contextualize the underpinnings of the assessment process and framework. The following are brief accounts by the authors to illustrate the importance of *testimonios* as a methodology for EL assessment practices and instruments.

As the first author found in his former work as a bilingual school psychologist, he witnessed how the language and culture of students and families were rarely considered or included in the pre-referral and referral process in special education, leading to overrepresentation of culturally and linguistically diverse student in special education programs. This experience also provided the significance and importance of all educators being knowledgeable about cultural and linguistic factors that could be affecting academic success for all students and for ELs in particular.

The second author, a former bilingual and ESL teacher at the elementary level, found that practices to assess ELs' conceptual knowledge about topics of study were in a language that the EL either did not understand or had limited language proficiency in, preventing them from fully engaging in tasks that required advanced English language-proficiency skills. In addition, based on the second author's prior experiences, assessments of ELs became essential ways to diagnose and establish correct placement of ELs in content learning that concluded in the application of effective practices to support ELs' linguistic and academic growth and progress.

HISTORY, PROCESS, AND ESSENTIAL ASSESSMENT COMPONENTS FOR ELS

When reflecting on the historical significance of assessment for ELs, it is important to revisit the role of assessment and the lack thereof in the identification and academic placement of ELs in the classroom. Missing elements regarding assessment have been treated in a dichotomous or compartmentalized way that disregards the connection between language and culture (Mercuri, 2012, p. 14). Issues that arise when this connection is disregarded are, for example, the lack of appropriate assessments to accurately evaluate

ELs, cultural bias in assessment development, and the misinterpretation of the assessment results (Liasidou, 2013, p. 12).

There have been approaches that include not only how language is assessed but also culture as well in the outcomes of assessment and student learning (Menchaca-López & López, 2008). This approach is a stark improvement on traditional, monocultural approaches in assessing ELs (Sanchez, 1932), but it is still considered a checklist approach that excludes the influence of a student's background in their learning. Moreover, a holistic approach to assessment that is conducted through interviews and observations would identify how an EL's ethnic identity and the acculturation process impact learning and assessment outcomes.

Cultural traits that assist in understanding and operationalizing a cultural validity framework include worldview, ethnic identity, and acculturation (López et al., 2005) and embed language, language development, and ultimately language proficiency. Worldview is "a culturally structured, systematic way looking at, perceiving, and interpreting various world realities" (Smedley & Smedley 2012, p. 16). Ethnic identity is considered the thoughts, feelings, and views of ourselves, our ethnic group, and others (Ponterotto & Pedersen, 1993). Acculturation is the process of individuals or groups maintaining their native culture while adopting new cultural traits (Cleveland & Xu 2019, p. 251).

It is crucial for educators and practitioners to understand the deep meaning of these cultural traits and how they may be operationalized within the practitioner, students, and their families. Worldview, ethnic identity, and acculturation and their implications on the assessment process uncover the cultural biases that may exist for ELs (Sattler et al., 2018). These constructs help practitioners understand themselves and how students may be understanding and processing information, situations, and interactions (Vázquez, 1997).

For example, acculturated traits, behaviors, and expectations, including acquiring advanced English language proficiency, may be unknown to the EL student and their family but are the expectations of the educational system (Vélez-Ibáñez & Greenberg, 1992, p. 330). Another example is the cultural values from a collective culture, such as humility, that may go unrecognized in a school system, where showing and/or communicating verbally what you know is expected and even rewarded.

Recognizing and comprehending these concepts and their implications in the assessment process, including cultural biases that may exist, can increase the awareness of discriminatory actions or practices in all phases of assessment of ELs (Kritkos et al., 2018, pp. 71–72). This process starts with assessment development, administration, scoring, and interpreting of results. These can have short- and long-term consequences for the educator, evaluator, EL students, and their families.

LANGUAGE ASSESSMENT AS A HOLISTIC APPROACH

To exemplify a holistic approach for an EL based on developing ongoing practices that have evolved to develop an assessment model is critical to development of an assessment process that considers the environmental contextual factors of the student experience. As presented in the historical portion of this chapter, testing for ELs has always been a point of contention, where misconceptions regarding language and culture are fueled by the lack of oversight on the sound implementation of this testing that has been proved to present further challenges (Linan-Thompson, 2010).

However, the assessment of ELs is the primary source for educators to make sound decisions addressing the progress and initiating the growth of ELs in both the areas of language and academic learning. For ELs, it is essential to understand that the student experience is made up of generational differences, variation in language, language-proficiency levels, and issues pertaining to race, ethnicity, and class (Vélez-Ibáñez & Greenberg, 1992). Therefore, for educators, this can be further explored as factors that affect the assessment practices for ELs.

In order to operationalize a holistic approach for ELs, teachers can engage their assessment practices by taking into account the different dimensions that can yield fruitful assessment results that address the linguistic and academic needs of ELs. For example, teachers can take into account the surrounding community of ELs such as environmental print, funds of knowledge, student prior experiences, generational levels, proficiency in their native and second language, and academic performance on formative and summative exams (Duckor & Holmberg, 2019, p. 47).

In order to understand the distinction between an EL's language proficiency or knowledge to use the language domains of listening, speaking, reading, and writing in fluent and meaningful ways, educators should understand that assessments for ELs should distinguish between language proficiency and academic content knowledge (Liasidou, 2013, p. 12). Moreover, educators should evaluate ELs based on the linguistic features of their first and second language and their proficiency in each language (Mercuri, 2012).

By understanding that distinction, teachers can understand their students' development in the different components of language (phonology, morphology, syntax) and identify areas where ELs can improve their English language development (Kritkos et al., 2018, p. 329). Based on this feedback, teachers can differentiate between proficiency levels in their instruction to provide linguistic accommodations in their lessons to assist in the pronunciation, fluency, comprehension, and meaning of an ELs' progression to increasing comprehension and communicative competence in English (Whyte, 2019).

POLICIES AND PRACTICES TOWARD
EL STUDENTS IN ASSESSMENTS

With every change in legislative reform, the identification and terminology used to federally identify an EL has transitioned. With the No Child Left Behind Act (NCLB) and prior reform efforts that used the term *limited English proficient* (LEP), to the current legislation of Every Student Succeeds Act (ESSA), in which the current federal term changed to *English learner* (EL), it is apparent that the federal government now hold states more accountable for the progress of ELs (Fensterwald, 2016). Yet, in the 21st century, we are continuing to pose the same concerns that George Sanchez (1932) proposed at the turn of the 20th century to understand the assessment of diverse students, yet expecting reliable and valid results.

The unfortunate outcome of the misuse of assessments for ELs has increased the under- and overrepresentation of ELs in federal and state programs (Liasidou, 2013, p. 12). This has resulted in misdiagnosis of ELs due to culture and language not being taken into consideration in assessment to measure development, administration, and results, and mismeasuring academic achievement, intelligence, speech and language, and personality (Hallahan et al., 2019).

A CONCEPTUAL CULTURAL VALIDITY FRAMEWORK

As indicated above, both language and culture are equally relevant to assessment and assessment outcomes for ELs. As discussed by DelliCarpini and Guler (2013, p. 126), language and culture are intertwined and lay the path toward inclusive assessment practices. The framework for testing ELs should encompass from the initial design, the language and cultural knowledge to accurately assess all areas currently valued in the educational system. A cultural validity framework authenticates and substantiates individual differences, encompassing both cultural and linguistic differences. Figure 9.1 illustrates the relationship between the essential components.

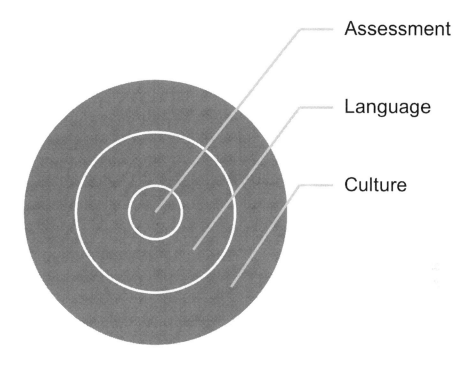

Assessment

Language

Culture

Figure 9.1. Conceptualization of a cultural validity framework. *Author created.*

Thus, under this framework, an EL's culture and language are viewed as embedded in the assessment processes and practices. Culture is considered in this framework as the overarching layer in this relationship that ensures inclusion of cultural constructs (López et al., 2005). Language is the next layer, containing the linguistic components inherent to all languages (e.g., phonology, morphology, syntax, semantics) that are used to comprehend and express meaningful communication to engage in learning the linguistic and cultural literacy practices found in multilingual and multicultural educational contexts (Kritkos et al., 2018, p. 329).

The cultural validity framework presents this embedded relationship that demonstrates language as an essential component of culture. Both are intertwined and are critical parts of any valid and reliable assessment for ELs. Rather than having students fit the assessment, we should assess ELs by taking into account their cultural and linguistic backgrounds and knowledge stemming from their environmental contexts (Vélez-Ibáñez & Greenberg, 1992).

RECOMMENDATIONS

The cultural validity framework allows educators and practitioners to contextualize critical consciousness (Valenzuela, 2016). As shown by López and colleagues (2020), critical consciousness "is the development of a deep awareness and critique of the historical roots and contemporary social dynamics that sustain the marginalization of most ML [multilingual] students" (p. 64). By having culture and language rooted in the assessment process, this allows opportunities to truly know and understand ELs and their families and to bring about effective practice.

This allows for a critical approach to developing evaluation tools for ELs and interpreting standardized norm-reference assessments within the environmental context of the students' cultural and linguistic background (Hallahan et al., 2019). It also acknowledges the need for more time for ELs learning a new language and/or acculturating (López & Davis, 2019), as well as other factors affecting assessment performance and outcomes. The cultural validity assessment framework applies to the use of alternative assessments and throughout the use of the Response to Intervention (RTI) process (Hallahan et al., 2019).

This becomes extremely critical as we enter a new era of online assessment for ELs. Technology and lack thereof are currently affecting how we address our testing needs with the increased use of different technological platforms that evaluate ELs' language proficiency and academic learning. Particularly in the 21st century, the addition of remote learning has also contributed to the increased use of instructional and evaluative ways to assess ELs (Goldstein, 2020).

It is recommended, particularly with the current emphasis on technology for learning, that all educators and practitioners working with ELs receive training and/or professional development in the theory and practice of a cultural validity framework. By committing to understand that it is everyone's responsibility when working with culturally and linguistically diverse learners such as ELs to understand and practice the model consistently. This assures advocacy and, ultimately, success for all students and their families.

REFERENCES

Bernal, D. D., Burciaga, R., & Carmona, J. F. (Eds.). (2017). *Chicana/Latina testimonios as pedagogical, methodological, and activist approaches to social justice.* Routledge.

Cleveland, M., & Xu, C. (2019). Multifaceted acculturation in multiethnic settings. *Journal of Business Research, 103*, 250–260.

DelliCarpini, M., & Guler, N. (2013). Success with ELLs: Assessing ELL students in mainstream classes: A new dilemma for the teachers. *The English Journal, 102*(3), 126–129.

Duckor, B., & Holmberg, C. (2019). 7 high-leverage formative assessment moves to support ELLs. *Educational Leadership, 77*(4), 46–52.

Fensterwald, J. (2016). *New federal law puts spotlight on English learners.* EdSource. https://edsource.org/2016/new-federal-law-puts-spotlight-on-english-learners /94222

Fuentes, E. H., & Pérez, M. A. (2016). Our stories are our sanctuary: *Testimonio* as a sacred space of belonging. *Association of Mexican American Educators Journal, 10*(2), 6–15.

Goldstein, D. (2020, March 13). Coronavirus is shutting schools. Is America ready for virtual learning? *New York Times.* https://www.nytimes.com/2020/03/13/us/virtual -learning-challenges.html

Hallahan, D. P., Kaufman, J. M., & Pullen, P. C. (2019). *Exceptional learners: An introduction to special education* (14th ed.). Pearson.

Kritkos, E. P., McLoughlin, J. A., & Lewis, R. B. (2018). *Assessing students with special needs* (8th ed.). Pearson.

Liasidou, A. (2013). Bilingual and special educational needs in inclusive classrooms: Some critical and pedagogical considerations. *Support for Student Learning, 28*(1), 16.

Linan-Thompson, S. (2010). Response to intervention, English language learners and disproportionate representation: The role of assessment. *Psicothema, 22*(4), 970–974.

Lopez, E. J., & Davis, M. T. (2019). A matter of time: English language learners and the RTI process. *Teacher Education Journal of South Carolina, 13*(1), 83–92.

López, E., Salas, L., & Flores, J. P. (2005). Hispanic preschool children: What about assessment and intervention? *Young Children, 60*(6), 48–54.

López, F., Desai, M., & Tintiangco-Cubales, A. (2020). Asset-based pedagogy: Student, family and community engagement for the academic and social-emotional learning of multilingual students. In *Improving education for multilingual and English learner students* (pp. 63–113). California Department of Education. https: //www.cde.ca.gov/sp/el/er/documents/mleleducation.pdf

Menchaca-López, E., & López, E. (2008). Acculturation in school-age students: The unseen factor. *Borderwalking Journal, 7*(1), 33–35.

Mercuri, S. P. (2012). Understanding the interconnectedness between language choices, cultural identity construction and school practices in the life of a Latina educator. *GIST Education and Learning Research Journal, 6*, 12–43.

Myers, L. J., Anderson, M., Lodge, T., Speight, S., & Queener, J. E. (2018). Optimal theory's contribution to understanding surmounting global challenges to humanity. *Journal of Black Psychology, 44*(8), 747–771.

National Research Council. (2011). *Allocating federal funds for state programs for English language learners.* National Academic Press.

Ponterotto, J. G., & Pedersen, P. B. (1993). *Preventing prejudice: A guide for counselors and educators.* SAGE.

Sanchez, G. I. (1932). Group differences and Spanish-speaking children—a critical review. *Journal of Applied Psychology, 16*(5), 549–558.

Sattler, J. M., Kitzie, M., & Oades-Sese, G. (2018). Culturally and linguistically diverse children. In J. M. Sattler (Ed.), *Assessment of children: Cognitive foundations and applications* (6th ed., pp. 137–182). Jerome M. Sattler.

Smedley, A., & Smedley, B. D. (2012). *Race in North America: Origin and evolution of a worldview* (4th ed.). Routledge.

U.S. Department of Education. (2018). *Our nation's English language learners: What are their characteristics.* https://www2.ed.gov/datastory/elcharacteristics/index.html

Valenzuela, A. (2016). *Growing critically conscious teachers: A social justice curriculum for educators of Latino/a youth.* Teachers College Press.

Vázquez, L. A. (1997). A systematic multicultural curriculum model: The pedagogical process. In D. B. Pope-Davis & H. L. K. Coleman (Eds.), *Multicultural counseling competencies: Assessment, education and training, and supervision* (pp. 159–183). SAGE.

Vélez-Ibáñez, C. G., & Greenberg, J. B. (1992). Formation and transformation of funds of knowledge among U.S.-Mexican households. *Anthropology & Education Quarterly, 23*(4), 313–335.

Whyte, S. (2019). Revisiting communicative competence in the teaching and assessment of language for specific purposes. *Language Education & Assessment, 2*(1), 1–19.

Chapter 10

Grade Level Placement of English Language Learners

Legal and Ethical Considerations

Mariola Krol

Social action begins with a vision to transform society and actively contribute to the development of awareness, knowledge, and tools for creating and sustaining change over a long period of time. It is a responsibility of a social justice leader to critically examine the practices of their organizations to identify policies, structures, and beliefs that create barriers to equitable opportunities and outcomes. Educators as social justice leaders must take action to foster change within their organizations and work to eliminate barriers with the goal of promoting a more just society.

The foundations of effective social justice leadership are rooted not only in legal but also in moral and ethical values. Law and ethics are inseparable aspects of problem-solving that leaders constantly encounter in school contexts. Some of the problems that school leaders encounter may be routine, structured problems; others may be more complex and present multiple options for solutions. School leaders are required to consider and solve all problems, including non-routine, ill-structured issues, by following the principles of social justice.

One educational issue that needs to be carefully considered from both legal and ethical perspectives, as it affects an individual's future, is grade-level placement of English language learners (ELLs) who enter the U.S. educational system. The question arises whether grade-level-placement determination for ELLs entering varying levels of U.S. schools should be based on the student's birthdate, or on prior schooling and academic readiness.

Although it is a general policy in several states to place newly entering ELLs in grade-level classes, some ELLs are placed in lower grades based on their lack of required skills. Lower grade-level placement may benefit younger students who attend elementary or middle schools. However, older students entering the high school system should be placed in age-based grade-level classes and provided adequate support to ensure their success.

Grade-level placement of ELLs often presents school leaders with a great challenge. Within the last decade, several districts throughout the nation have experienced an influx of diverse students from various educational systems outside of the United States. The new entrants enrich the cultural mosaic of American schools by bringing in a variety of lived experiences, languages, cultures, and values. They are often considered an asset, and many districts have committed to building on the diversity of the student body. District administrators recognize diversity as a vital element in the district's cultural enrichment.

Many districts try to embrace the demographic changes and attempt to serve each part of the student population based on equity and social justice, but at the same time they are faced with dilemmas that require careful consideration. Several ELLs who are entering U.S. schools are older than 14 or 15, which is the age of an average high school freshman. At the same time, the maximum age limit for a person to attend a public high school is 20 or 21. Therefore, students in their late teens have the legal right to enroll in a public school despite the number of completed years of schooling, high school credits they have previously acquired, or the level of English language proficiency.

Many of the new entrants differ from average American teenagers in several ways. Many of them were treated as adults in their countries. While enjoying adult privileges, they were often burdened with adult responsibilities, which forced them to mature very quickly. The financial situation of their families may have caused them to drop out of school in order to work and earn an income to support the family. As a result of their interrupted education, they lack not only credits required for graduation but also general academic proficiency necessary to be successful in school settings.

Some students have been traumatized by crossing the border illegally all by themselves. Several had been detained for months before they were able to reach their families in the United States. When they arrive in the United States, they often have to seek employment in addition to attending school. As a result of these experiences, they may feel disconnected from their much younger and often less mature classmates, many of whom have lived sheltered lives and have not experienced the same kinds of obstacles and challenges.

Upon entering the new school, students arriving from countries outside of the United States are usually given an identification test to assess their

English language level. If a student is a beginning English learner and lacks high school credits from the home country, despite their age, he or she is often automatically placed in ninth grade without any further consideration. Although most states follow the rule of placing students in appropriate grade-level classes based on their birthdates, this rule does not often apply to ELLs.

Placing older students in ninth grade, where the majority of students are 14–15 years of age, causes numerous problems that may negatively impact the learning atmosphere. There is a great difference in maturity level between the newly entering older students and the rest of the class. Having enjoyed the privileges of adulthood at home, the students often find it difficult to adapt to school rules and to being treated like children. In addition, younger peers who notice their maturity may see them as role models and act to impress them, which leads to a disrupted learning atmosphere.

Acquiring English language skills, trying to meet academic standards, and adjusting to the school rules and the new culture present a challenge that older new entrants often find too difficult to overcome. Furthermore, they tend to feel humiliated by the lower grade-level placement and experience a lack of motivation. Therefore, soon after enrolling in school, they often drop out, having no hope for fulfilling their American dream of getting a high school diploma and pursuing a college degree. They may gear toward low-paying jobs that do not require English proficiency or specific skills.

Grade-level placement of older ELLs who lack English language skills and high school credits required for graduation presents decision-makers with noteworthy ethical and legal issues. Therefore, several agencies have attempted to create decision-making models and have offered reasonable solutions revolving around a careful consideration of both ethical and legal principles.

In moral philosophy, *deontology* is used to refer to rules or constraints that are moral imperatives. These moral imperatives command action of a specific type in appropriate circumstances without reference to reasons or consequences. Some of these rules are to treat others as you want to be treated, be fair, provide equity for all students, and respect other people's values. Rules like these should be followed regardless of anyone monitoring educators or threatening them with consequences.

Deontological beliefs are in alignment with solutions based on the Interstate School Leaders Licensure Consortium's (ISLLC) conceptual framework, which provides a foundation for approaching educational dilemmas. ISLLC standards are designed to provide guidance regarding responsibilities of school and district leaders. According to one of the standards regarding ethics and professional norms, effective educational leaders should promote every student's academic success and well-being by acting ethically and according to professional norms.

Another ISLLC standard relates to equity and cultural responsiveness in creating a positive school climate, curriculum planning, and designing instructional practices. The standard points out that the foundations of effective educational leadership include striving for equity of educational opportunity. Culturally responsive practices should ensure that students' cultures are valued and built on as assets. This standard speaks to the consideration of students' diverse cultural and educational experiences in decision-making.

Following the above principles, decision-makers must ensure that students who enter the U.S. educational system are given an equitable educational opportunity and are placed in grade-level classes based on their birthdate. Such placement will provide the opportunity for older new entrants to interact with their peers without lowering their self-esteem by placing them in a lower grade level with much younger students. In addition to core academic classes, support in the form of tutoring and resource rooms should be offered to these students to provide opportunities for English language and academic skills development.

Also, districts that have experienced an influx of students with interrupted formal education should develop special programs that address the needs of ELLs who are expected to reach the age of 21 before being able to meet graduation criteria in terms of the required credits and assessments. In these programs, students would not have to face the challenges of rigorous classes that focus on state assessments, but instead effectively learn communication and career skills to prepare them for future lives.

While offering instruction to improve the students' English proficiency skills, such programs could focus on civic engagement, life science, customer service, hygiene, and technical skills to eventually prepare the students for an independent career outside of the school setting if the decision is made that a student will not be able to meet the required graduation criteria. The program would allow older ELLs to remain in school while eliminating either the challenge of being placed in a lower-grade class with much younger peers or the struggle of being in a grade-level class when they lack the required skills.

As the new entrant's future is being determined by the grade-level placement upon entering the American education system, several decision-makers should be involved to carefully examine each case and make the right decision. The grade placement should be decided in a collaborative process by the language specialist, school administrators, general classroom teacher, guidance counselor, the student's parents, and sometimes a school psychologist or a social worker.

Various assessment factors should also be taken into consideration when making the decision regarding grade-level placement: for example, the student's age, prior schooling, socioemotional and academic readiness skills, achievement levels in math and language arts, as well as language proficiency. Not all decision-makers need to participate in each case, but if the student's individual situation involves a trauma—for example, escaping from a war-torn zone or separating from the rest of the family—the input from a psychologist or a social worker may be necessary.

Several laws have been written to regulate the grade-level placement of English language learners upon entering the U.S. educational system. These laws define national and state regulations, case law, district policy, as well as local district practice. One such law is *Lau v. Nichols* of 1974, based on the U.S. Supreme Court case in which the court unanimously decided that the lack of supplemental language instruction in public schools for students with limited English proficiency violated the Civil Rights Act of 1964.

The Supreme Court decision stated that children must acquire basic communication and academic English language skills before they can adequately participate in an educational program. It further stated that it is unconstitutional to place ELLs in lower grades. As a result of the law, school districts have been required to provide students with educational opportunities that are appropriate for their situation as new entrants into the school system.

Some states have also issued laws that offer solutions to the issue of grade-level placement of ELLs. For example, the New York State Commissioner's Regulation Part 154 requires student placement in a bilingual education or English as a New Language program within 10 school days after initiating the identification process. However, according to the regulation, schools are allowed up to 1 year to determine grade placement for new entrants with a low literacy level in the home language. Upon enrollment, the school is required to assign the student to a grade level based on the administrator's best judgement.

The temporary grade level must be reported in the first year of enrollment if the student has not yet been enrolled a full academic year. Before the end of the second year of enrollment, the school evaluates the student and determines the appropriate grade level based on the student's scheduled coursework for the semester. New York State Commissioner's Regulation 154 further states that students cannot be placed in a lower grade or retained solely based on language proficiency.

Although several factors point to the rationality of grade-level placement determined by the student's birthdate, some argue that prior schooling and academic readiness rather than birthdate should be taken into consideration. As a result, students may be placed in grades lower than their birthdate would normally determine.

Proponents of such decisions point out that the student's deficits in prior academic background, level of social and emotional development, limited ability, and low readiness skills often resulting from incongruent curricula may negatively impact academic success, self-esteem, and attitude toward school. Consequently, such proponents claim that elementary or middle school students who are ELLs should be placed in a lower grade if initial assessments of their prior schooling indicate curricular gaps.

Placing students in lower grades than their birthdates affords these students the time to acquire necessary skills and foundations to achieve academic success while also developing their English proficiency. They may be able to adjust to the new education system and learn the study skills that they may have not acquired in their home country and that are essential to the student's academic success. Periodic progress assessments can be utilized to determine if subsequent grade-placement adjustments, such as reassignment to grade by birthdate, are warranted.

The theory of relativism can be used to justify why an arbitrary decision regarding grade-level placement of students with limited English proficiency may not be the best solution. Relativism is a philosophical concept based on the belief that knowledge, truth, and morality exist in relation to culture, society, or historical context, and are not absolute. As a result, points of view have no absolute truth within themselves, but rather only relative, subjective value according to differences in perception by different people.

Jean-Paul Sartre, who claimed that subjectivity is the beginning of ethics, said that the greatest evil of which we are capable is to treat as abstract that which is concrete. Sartre found moral significance in specific situations and real persons rather than generalizations and formulas. As a result, cultural setting and circumstances should determine the decision-making, and since there is no absolute right and wrong, the truth should always be viewed in relation to a particular frame of reference.

Several ethical issues—for example, social and emotional impact, peer interaction, and access to age-appropriate curriculum—are involved when deciding the student's grade-level placement. The foundations of democratic society guarantee the commitment to including all students regardless of their differences. Equality is one of the guiding principles of the Declaration of Independence. However, equality means treating people the same way if they are the same. If people are different in some relevant ways, decisions regarding these people should revolve around inclusion and equity rather than equality.

In a school setting, the principle of equity over equality can justify different treatment of such students because their needs are different. Therefore, each case should be thoroughly examined, and decisions should be carefully made, since the student's future is at stake. Placing students in grade-level classes in some situations, especially high school settings where peer interaction plays a crucial role in the student's success, may be the best solution, while in other settings, like elementary or middle school, it may serve the students better when they are placed in a lower grade because they are given additional time to meet general education standards.

The unquestionable guiding principle of acting in an ethical manner should lay at the foundation of every decision-making process in order to promote every student's success. Understanding and applying not only legal but also ethical frameworks in educational problem-solving is an essential building block of competent school leadership.

Chapter 11

Characteristics of English Learners

Daniela DiGregorio

The growing population of English learners (ELs) has reached approximately 4 million in U.S. public schools (National Center for Education Statistics, 2020). As a result, districts are hiring more English as a Second Language (ESL) teachers, revising ESL or ELD (English language development) programs, and providing professional development on how to accommodate instruction for ELs.

ELs are students who are in the process of acquiring English as their second or additional language. In order to identify ELs in K–12 educational settings, all parents must complete a home language survey, which determines if a student should be evaluated for ESL services. After students are found eligible for services, an ESL teacher enrolls them into an ESL/ELD program and provides instruction as well as other support to assist their needs.

Some states changed their ESL program that focuses on teaching English to students with age-appropriate literacy skills to an ELD program in which ELs with limited literacy skills not only develop their English language proficiency but also learn strategies to succeed in content areas. According to the Pennsylvania Department of Education, the content-area teachers are responsible for developing ELs' literacy in the particular content, and ESL teachers focus on English instruction, which is driven by language,

> but it draws from general education content as a vehicle for instruction in order to contextualize language learning. It must be codified in a dedicated and planned curriculum specifically designed to develop the English language proficiency of ELs so that they are able to use English in social and academic settings and access challenging academic standards. (Commonwealth of Pennsylvania, 2021, para. 5)

Throughout the school year, ESL teachers administer at least one standardized test that determines ELs' level of English proficiency. ACCESS for ELLs 2.0 was developed by the World-Class Instructional Design and Assessment (WIDA) and is one of the national standardized tests for ELs. WIDA is a consortium of 35 states, and it designs high-quality standards and assessments for ELs. ACCESS test scores provide information about students' English proficiency levels in reading, writing, listening, and speaking.

There are six WIDA English-proficiency levels: (1) entering, (2) emerging, (3) developing, (4) expanding, (5) bridging, and (6) reaching (Board of Regents of the University of Wisconsin System, 2020). The WIDA consortium also developed "Can Do Descriptors," which illustrate what English learners are able to accomplish at different English-proficiency levels. A chart of Can Do Descriptors is an essential guide for ESL teachers as well as content-area teachers. WIDA levels and Can Do Descriptors assist teachers in providing accommodations and differentiated instruction for ELs.

Many countries and languages are represented in U.S. schools. According to the U.S. Department of Education (2014–2015), over 3 million ELs speak Spanish; other highly represented languages are Arabic, Chinese, Vietnamese, Somali, Hmong, Russian, Haitian Creole, Tagalog, and Korean (NCES, 2020). ELs entering U.S. schools are at various stages of culture shock, and their acculturation is a timely process. Some ELs never fully accept the dominant culture. ELs can be categorized into five different groups, described below.

REFUGEE ENGLISH LEARNERS

The first group consists of refugee ELs who were born in a foreign country where their living situation became too dangerous. As a result, refugee families fled their native country, lived in refugee camps, and sought asylum to resettle in another country. According to the UN Refugee Agency,

> A refugee is someone who has been forced to flee his or her country because of persecution, war or violence. A refugee has a well-founded fear of persecution for reasons of race, religion, nationality, political opinion or membership in a particular social group. Most likely, they cannot return home or are afraid to do so. War and ethnic, tribal and religious violence are leading causes of refugees fleeing their countries. (USA for UNHCR, 2020, para. 1)

Many refugees come to the United States from countries like Syria, Nepal, Iraq, Burma, Nigeria, Ethiopia, or the Democratic Republic of Congo, to name a few.

The significant difference between refugee and immigrant families is that refugees have no other choice but to leave their native country in order to survive. Refugee students experience many challenges in new educational settings due to prior limited schooling, low literacy levels, poor living conditions, war trauma, or post-traumatic stress. Refugees' acculturation process might be slower due to the challenges mentioned above or the fact that they had to accept asylum in a country that was not their choice.

School administrators and teachers can help refugee students by developing effective newcomer programs, offering sheltered instruction, providing after-school tutoring, creating a positive learning environment, and educating school staff about culture shock and post-traumatic stress.

IMMIGRANT ENGLISH LEARNERS

The second group includes immigrant students who were born abroad like refugees, but their parents or caregivers voluntarily decided to leave their native country in a search of better life. Many immigrants arrive from Mexico, India, China, Philippines, Vietnam, Cuba, the Dominican Republic, and other countries (Wright, 2019).

Some immigrant students may bring with them a wealth of knowledge and easily transfer high literacy and learning strategies skills from previous school environments. This is called *positive transfer* (Wright, 2019). When students use *positive transfer* during their second-language acquisition, they will show significant progress. Such English learners should not attend a slow-paced ESL/ELD program but rather should get the ESL teacher's assistance to accelerate their second-language acquisition.

On the other side, some students might find learning English challenging, especially if their native language is significantly distant from the target language. Chinese, Korean, Russian, and Arabic are considered much more distant from English than Romance languages such as Spanish or French. Teachers might notice *negative transfer* when English learners transfer their native-language writing style, syntax, and grammar into their English essays (Wright, 2019).

Students who have lived in the United States for one to two years are called *newcomers.* Some newcomers will be highly schooled and will adjust faster to a new school environment, while newcomers with low English and native literacy skills will take more time to adjust and show improvement. Often, *newcomers* who are beginning to learn English will go through a so-called *silent period.* During the silent period, newcomers are developing listening and comprehension skills but remain silent and should not be forced to talk. The silent period can last weeks or months depending on each person.

All teachers, not just ESL teachers, must be familiar with effective teaching strategies that allow ELs to participate in classes. Using scaffolding strategies and tools such as visuals and graphic organizers is highly successful, as well as differentiated instruction for varying language levels and the use of informal assessments.

MIGRANT ENGLISH LEARNERS

The third group is composed of migrant students. Their parents are migrant workers who frequently relocate in search of available jobs in the agricultural and fishing industries. About 90% of migrant children are Latino and 34% are ELs (Lundy-Ponce, 2010). Although migrant workers want better educational opportunities for their children, migrant students typically get little help from their parents, who have a low educational background. Frequent moves during the school year and many socioeconomic disadvantages have a negative impact on migrant students. As a result, these students have the highest rate of school dropouts.

Migrant English learners deal with more challenges than other English learners do. Some of the major obstacles are high mobility, acute poverty, health hazards, educational disadvantages, and social alienation (Lundy-Ponce, 2010). In addition, older students are expected to work in the fields after school hours, which prevents them from attending after-school tutoring or extracurricular classes.

Migrant ELs are often "Students with Limited or Interrupted Formal Education" (SLIFEs). According to Calderon (2008), these students might have experienced one of the patterns below:

- have had two or more years of interrupted education in their native country;
- have attended U.S. schools, then moved to their native country, and after a period of time came back to the United States;
- have attended U.S. schools in one location and moved to another location in the United States with gaps in school attendance; or
- have attended U.S. schools since kindergarten but have literacy gaps due to insufficient instruction. (Robertson & Lafond, n.d.)

SLIFE students will go through high levels of stress and frustration because they are far behind their classmates. They are also at high risk of dropping out of school. School staff can assist these students by implementing newcomer centers, offering flexible scheduling, increasing sheltered instruction, and providing intensive literacy instruction (Spaulding et al., 2004).

In addition, educational staff need to be aware of possible solutions that can be beneficial to migrant students. It is essential that completed student documentation is transferred to a new school district in a timely manner, and that teachers provide continuation of former curricula. Educating migrant families about online instruction and supplying them with digital resources such as Chromebooks, educational software, and internet access is extremely important.

INTERNATIONALLY ADOPTED ENGLISH LEARNERS

The fourth group comprises internationally adopted children who were adopted during their school years. These children were born in a foreign country and were placed in orphanages if their parents or legal guardians could not take care of them. American parents adopt these children, move them from their native country to the United States, and enroll them in U.S. schools. Countries with high international adoption rates are China, India, Ethiopia, South Korea, Ukraine, and Vietnam (Selman, 2013).

Commonly, internationally adopted children acquire English faster as a result of full English immersion and support from adoptive parents; however, some international adoptees might have physical disabilities or learning delays due to poor nutrition and inadequate living conditions in the orphanages.

Younger children who were adopted before the age of 12 typically experience *subtractive bilingualism.* Wright (2019) stated *subtractive bilingualism* occurs when students' second language (English) replaces their native language (Russian, Chinese, Vietnamese, etc.). Their full immersion in an English-only environment and lack of connection to their native language prevents them from maintaining their native language.

Older students who were adopted after the age of 12 will be able to maintain their native language despite their full English immersion. If international adoptees had sufficient schooling in their native country and are encouraged to continue reading and writing in their native language, they will experience *additive bilingualism* (Wright, 2019). Successful *additive bilingualism* means that international adoptees will be able to add their second language without replacing their native language.

Education staff should provide adoptive families with informative resources and communicate with adoptive parents and children about how to make the school environment and class assignments more adoption friendly. ESL teachers must communicate regularly with adoptive parents about children's progress and discuss any concerns.

GENERATION 1.5 ENGLISH LEARNERS

The fifth group of English learners is *Generation 1.5*. Students who belong into this group are U.S. residents or citizens who were born and educated in the United States, but their first or dominant language is not English. In some cases, English might be a primary language, but it is not well developed because the home environment is bilingual, or their parents struggle themselves with English skills. This also applies to students living in Native American tribes. The term *Generation 1.5* is connected to students' cultural feelings of being between the first and second generations of immigrants (Fleischer, 2017).

ELs who are Generation 1.5 students face challenges such as less knowledge of grammar rules, limited phonemic awareness, or weak exposure to reading in English, which has a negative influence on their writing skills. Although they are fluent English speakers, they are often identified as having weaker literacy skills and typically struggle with academic English, especially in their reading and writing assignments (Stanford University, 2020).

There are differences between Generation 1.5 students and typical ESL students. Teachers should be aware that Generation 1.5 students have excellent oral skills but experience gaps in their grammar, parts of speech, and subject-verb agreement when writing essays. As a result, Generation 1.5 students might not be eligible for ESL/ELD services but will need assistance in mainstream classes. Singhal (2004) suggested that teachers provide detailed feedback so that students understand how to revise their writing. In addition, teachers need to review grammar rules and provide study guides of parts of speech.

English learners are diverse students who attend schools in all 50 states in the United States. They have various cultural backgrounds and different literacy skills. Those teachers who instruct ELs must get to know their students very well.

Teachers of ELs should collect data about students' primary language, former schooling, literacy practices, and cultural background. Based on this information, as well as ACCESS testing and other informal assessments, teachers will be able to focus on ELs' needs and provide appropriate accommodations. By knowing their cultural identity, socioeconomic background, linguistic challenges, and former educational systems, all teachers will be able to develop better strategies for effective instruction for their English learners.

REFERENCES

Board of Regents of the University of Wisconsin System. (2020). *WIDA: ACCESS for ELLs.* https://wida.wisc.edu/assess/access

Calderon, M. (2008). Innovative policies and practices for developing teachers to work with English language learners [Conference presentation]. ETS 2008 English Language Learners Symposium. http://www.ets.org/Media/Conferences _and_Events/pdf/ELLsympsium/Calderon.pdf

Commonwealth of Pennsylvania. (2021). *Educating English learners: ELD delivered by ESL teachers.* Pennsylvania Department of Education. https://www .education.pa.gov/Teachers%20-%20Administrators/Curriculum/English%20As %20A%20Second%20Language/Pages/default.aspx

Fleischer, C. (2017). *ESL, ELL, Generation 1.5—why are these terms important?* NCTE. https://ncte.org/blog/2017/09/esl-ell-generation-1-5-why-are-these-terms -important

Lundy-Ponce, G. (2010). *Migrant students: What we need to know to help them succeed.* ¡Colorín Colorado! https://www.colorincolorado.org/article/migrant-students -what-we-need-know-help-them-succeed

National Center for Education Statistics. (2020). *English language learners in public schools.* https://nces.ed.gov/programs/coe/indicator_cgf.asp

Robertson, K., & Lafond, S. (n.d.). *How to support ELL students with interrupted formal education (SIFEs).* ¡Colorín Colorado! https://www.colorincolorado.org/ article/how-support-ell-students-interrupted-formal-education-sifes

Selman, P. (2013). *Key tables for intercountry adoption: Receiving states 2003–2012. States of Origin 2003–2011.* Newcastle University.

Singhal, M. (2004). Academic writing and generation 1.5: Pedagogical goals and instructional issues in the college composition classroom. *The Reading Matrix, 4*(3), 1–13. http://www.readingmatrix.com/articles/singhal/article2.pdf

Spaulding, S., Carolino, B., & Amen, K. (2004). Immigrant students and secondary school reform: Compendium of best practices. CCSSO. Files.eric.ed.gov/fulltext/ ED484705.pdf

Stanford University. (2020). *Teaching writing: 1.5 generation and ESL.* https:// teachingcommons.stanford.edu/teachingwriting/pwr-guide/teaching-multilingual -students/generation-15-and-esl

USA for UNHCR. (2020). *What is a refugee?* https://www.unrefugees.org/refugee -facts/what-is-a-refugee

U.S. Department of Education. (2014–2015). *Most common non-English languages spoken by English learners.* https://www2.ed.gov/datastory/el-characteristics/index .html#three

Wright, W. (2019). *Foundations for teaching English language learners: Research, theory, policy and practice* (3rd ed.). Caslon.

Chapter 12

Fluidity of Diversity

Reshaping How Educators Understand English Language Learners' Needs in the Classroom

Dorota Silber-Furman and Andrea Arce-Trigatti

This chapter is designed to help practicing teachers, community activists, teacher educators, and administrators engage with distinct diversity and multicultural theories that can enhance the learning environments of ELLs. The purpose of this chapter is to present a holistic approach to English language learning that incorporates the journey from theory to practice as it reflects the concept of fluidity in learning. The idea for this chapter grew out of community activist work that centered on a unique interpretation of diversity in the sense of its fluidity.

Fluidity represents the ever-changing experiences and backgrounds that students bring to learning. This shapes their interpretation, internalization, and view of the curricular content that is presented. The fluidity construct, in terms of diversity in learning and teaching, has become a central component of the most effective practices for all English language learners (ELLs) via the work conducted by the authors with various community organizations, including:

- the Upper Cumberland ELL Adult Learning Courses Program;
- the Tennessee Chapter for the National Association for Multicultural Education;
- the National Association for Multicultural Education;
- IMPACT Leadership, IMPACT Cookeville; and
- the Eta Nu Chapter of Kappa Delta Pi (KDP) International Honor Society.

All of these organizations have leveraged an understanding of fluidity to promote initiatives of leadership, excellence, and community outreach in the form of language acquisition for diverse communities.

This approach is primarily anchored in the following theories: Crenshaw's (1991) intersectionality theory, Krashen's (2013) Monitor Model, and Cummins's (2000) Basic Interpersonal Communicative Skills (BICS) and Cognitive Academic Language Proficiency (CALP). Together, these provide a framework for understanding language acquisition through the lens of fluidity in learning that intentionally incorporates students' diverse backgrounds. By adopting a model wherein diversity and learning are considered fluid concepts, this deepens educators' understanding of how critical components of ELLs' identity formation influences their engagement and motivation with language acquisition.

THE NEED FOR A HOLISTIC MODEL
TO ELL EDUCATION

A holistic model for ELL education embodies the belief that diversity is a dynamic and rich concept that includes a multitude of human experiences that are influenced by a myriad of individual qualities. A holistic diversity definition that can guide teaching and learning experiences was developed throughout work with the organizations listed above. As part of this definition, diversity is recognized as a platform of opportunity to discover, explore, and understand distinct and dissimilar viewpoints shaped by individual and collective experiences.

In terms of diversity and inclusion, these can be embodied as conscious practices and fundamental goals at which educators should aim with ongoing efforts. In this framework, diversity is thus deeply rooted in civic action and global citizenship. To this end, it is believed that inclusive learning communities are invaluable to the idiosyncratic comprehension of teaching and learning and how it applies to ELLs' ever-changing learning contexts.

Such a community will inevitably contribute to ELLs' understanding of lifelong learning and will impact their ability to become culturally competent change agents, leaders, and citizens for this global society, representative of this holistic framework. This conceptualization of diversity is not perfect, as it reflects a cross-section of this belief within a specific point in time; however, as diversity is fluid, this definition should also change, adapt, and evolve. For ELLs, the adoption of this definition holds implications for the way fluidity is understood in terms of identity and language.

Fluidity of Identity

St. Pierre (1997) proposed that lived experiences are complicated and entangled, creating multiple folds of perception or even data, given meaning through language. She points out that language limits how knowledge is constructed because what we know is complex and multidimensional. Effectively, the claim that language influences what we know also implies that language determines the identity we develop within the social norms that we navigate.

Many ELL students struggle not only with lingual identity but also with the cultural identity and sense of belonging attached to their status as immigrants. The legal status that several ELL students hold is reflective of their journey: some are legal residents, some are not, and some are perpetually navigating immigration limbo. Knowledge, then, is a powerful medium that shapes and is shaped by the lived experiences of those who actively consume, internalize, reconstruct, and create it.

Individuals are situated within specific social, cultural, historical, and economic contexts that inform these lived experiences, influence their ability to critique and analyze knowledge as teachers and students, and shape their acceptance or rejection in society. In this respect, the identity development of ELL students, as associated with their language and immigration status, is in flux or, as denoted in this chapter, fluid.

Fluidity of Language

The WIDA (2020) Consortium is an educational entity that developed English language-proficiency standards in 2004 and provides language support to ELLs in 41 states, territories, and federal agencies. WIDA's mission clearly outlines a positive attitude to serve the ELL student population: "WIDA advances academic language development and academic achievement for children and youth who are culturally and linguistically diverse through high quality standards, assessments, research and professional learning for educators" (para. 5). In the English-proficiency standards, WIDA listed five language-development stages in categories of listening, speaking, reading, and writing, which include: Entering, Emerging, Developing, Expending, and Bridging. These offer a holistic understanding of language acquisition.

WIDA (2014), however, points out that language development is dependent on many social, academic, and developmental factors such as: "student personality, language exposure, instructional design, service delivery, scaffolding, models for language" (p. 5). In understanding this principle, the holistic framework of the fluidity of diversity strives to facilitate such a learning process to integrate the multiplicity of experiences that contribute to student learning.

The shaping of knowledge is therefore meant to empower those in learning communities to be global citizens and leaders within any learning environment.

KEY THEORIES

Bauer and colleagues (2018) indicated that "research increasingly recognizes that bilingualism is dynamic and flexible"; however, pedagogy does not "always reflect the fluid nature of language" (p. 22). This section presents the key learning theories that assisted in developing the holistic framework for the fluidity of diversity. Connections to intersectionality and how language shapes student learning identities are featured.

Crenshaw's Intersectionality Theory

Some variables that may influence school performance include diversity in religion and beliefs, parents' education level, parents' proficiency in English, socioeconomic status, abilities/disabilities, learning styles, time in the United States, immigration status, educational background (students with interrupted formal education), and literacy in the home language. Due to the continual intersection of these variables, Crenshaw (1991) developed the theory of intersectionality, wherein the concept of a multifaceted and fluid perception of one's social identity is argued to reflect the true nature of the complexity of diversity.

Crenshaw (1991) offered the following:

> Race, gender, and other identity categories are most often treated in mainstream liberal discourse as vestiges of bias or domination. . . . The problem with identity politics is not that it fails to transcend difference, as some critics charge, but rather the opposite—that it frequently conflates or ignores intragroup differences. (p. 1242)

Intersectionality offers that these social problems are a result of the dynamics that arise from the interpretations of the intersections of these struggles. This provides a theoretical foundation by which to engage with learning theories that are related to the intersections of language and culture and provide insight for educators to remember that ELLs hold diverse strengths and needs at these intersections.

Krashen's Monitor Model

Krashen's (2013) Monitor Model in the field of second-language acquisition explains that the dynamics of language processes are inherently intertwined with the identity development of the learner and the surrounding environment. Krashen (2013) highlighted that "if the acquirer is anxious, has low self-esteem, does not consider himself or herself to be a potential member of the group that speaks the language," then language acquisition will be impaired and "the block, the affective filter, will keep it out" (p. 4). He further emphasized that comprehensible input is an especially important component of a student's language acquisition.

Students learn when they understand messages; when students cannot decipher messages and create meaning from these exchanges, language acquisition is interrupted. As this relates to intersectionality and the fluidity of language, it can be discerned that when students feel welcome, understand the language of their surroundings, and can navigate through meaning-making, their identity as a student is being built up rather than dismantled.

Cummins's BICS and CALP

Cummins (2000) added to this with his discussion of English in which he explored how much proficiency in a language was necessary for a student to actively participate in the lesson and be successful in school. In reflecting about language learning and language proficiency, he shed light on the "fundamental distinction between conversational and academic aspects of language proficiency" (p. 58).

He asserted that there was a language gap between students' attainment of social and academic English; social language proficiency was developed within 2 years, while academic language needed 5–7 years of lingual exposure. The terms *Basic Interpersonal Communication Skills* (BICS) and *Cognitive Academic Language Proficiency* (CALP) are often referred to in his work. These concepts also provide insight into how language acquisition influences language-identity development, again reflective of the intersections of the fluidity of these notions.

For example, students develop the identity of social speaker, conversational speaker, and social media user, which are inherently different from elements related to the identity of a scholar or an academically proficient individual based on the way they communicate. The role of the teacher, then, is to foster the best of both worlds in order to make a student successful and continue growing both socially and academically.

APPLICATIONS IN THE CLASSROOM

Educators rely on daily classroom applications and practices to actively engage ELLs and foster academic success by integrating them into a larger learning community. Understanding the applications of these theories in the form of instructional strategies and effective language processes is paramount to developing a holistic and fluid pedagogy. In this section, these concepts, as well as curricular examples, are detailed.

Instructional Strategies

As noted, Crenshaw's (1991) sociological theory of intersectionality offers a comprehensive framework for evaluating and implementing the fluidity of a learning environment, such as ELLs' classroom space. In understanding ELLs' multifaceted identities and the various social, geographical, political, economic, historical, and cultural components that could influence learning, this provides an avenue for lesson planning and teaching that is receptive both to students' unique styles of learning and to their backgrounds.

This theory presents the core of the holistic approach that is presented in this chapter and provides a way to connect other theories that are conducive to diversity and inclusive practices and that ultimately guide ELL students at all levels to language-learning success. In terms of application, intersectionality is useful in lesson planning to identify gaps in the pedagogical practices being leveraged. This implies that educators need to be cognizant when using a multitude of strategies to incorporate learner styles and address the needs of all ELLs to help language-acquisition progress.

Effective Language Processes

As noted, language acquisition happens when a message is presented in such a way that the student is able to understand/comprehend what is being stated in the target language. To illustrate, Cloud and colleagues (2009) stated,

> When ELLs learn English, they learn more than the sounds, words, and grammatical patterns that make up English. They also learn how to use English in socially appropriate and effective ways. Most important, they learn how to be a fully functioning and valued members of their peer group. (pp. 10–11)

It is important that in the classroom with ELLs, the teacher will explicitly break down new cultural forms and patterns. Teachers must be aware that the students, while acquiring the new language, are also acquiring the new culture; thus, "cultural scaffolding" (Cloud et al., 2009) is essential for language comprehension.

In the classroom, the focus therefore needs to be on elements from Krashen's (1987) Monitor Model—including acquisition-learning hypothesis, natural-order hypothesis, monitor hypothesis, comprehensible input, and affective-filter hypothesis—and how these theories work in practice for ELLs. For instance, the comprehensible input can be transmitted via visuals, Asher's Total Physical Response (TPR) where movements and/or visuals are present, speech modification (slower and more announced), realia (representation of vocabulary by real objects), and culturally relevant activities.

Curricular Examples

Applying this holistic approach, which is rooted in diversity and multicultural theory, will ultimately aid in the implementation of research-based practices beneficial for ELLs. Coupling these theories to practice thus provides a foundation by which curriculum aligned with the concept of fluidity of diversity can be created. Examples of this application are listed below.

HOW TO TEACH GRAMMAR

In teaching grammar to ELLs, it is important to teach exactly that—*grammar*. Two pedagogical objectives guide this approach: (1) ensuring that the grammar instruction is to ELLs' level of comprehension and not intimidating, and (2) using texts and sentences with words of low complexity (Tier I vocabulary). The first objective can be achieved by organizing grammatical instruction in English tenses on one notebook page. Being able to review these guidelines on one page helps to visualize the simplicity and logic of language instruction (Arce-Trigatti & Silber-Furman, 2022).

For the second objective, teachers can then develop three sentences per tense with simple lexicon (a statement, a question, and a negative statement). The sentences create almost mathematical formulas per tense that the ELLs can easily reproduce by replacing the original sentences' vocabulary with their own words. These pedagogical objectives help ELLs to understand the fluidity of language by visualizing word exchanges, grammatical parameters, and academic communication as malleable. This further encourages ELL success through knowledge-building, as they can easily participate in this activity, integrating their voice into the curriculum.

ILLUSTRATING DIFFERENT PERSPECTIVES

Diverse perspectives are essential and comprise the central tenet of the conceptualization of diversity as fluid. One activity that can help students and teachers alike to understand this concept is the Bicycle Activity. For this lesson, students must first draw what comes to mind when they think of a bicycle. After everyone has completed their drawing, students are paired and asked to predict what their partners have drawn. The class then engages in a group discussion about larger patterns found.

This discussion reveals that students typically present their bicycles from similar perspectives that reflect a two-dimensional view, from the side, with two wheels, with a saddle and handlebars. To conclude the discussion, a presentation of bicycles drawn from all angles is presented. These new drawings often highlight overlooked perspectives related to bicycle designs. This myriad of drawings is meant to emphasize that shared perspectives often omit interesting conceptualizations of the same idea, linking back to the idea that diversity is conceptually fluid (Arce-Trigatti & Silber-Furman, 2022).

By educating, empowering, and engaging community members and stakeholders through effective diversity and inclusion practices, learning spaces can be developed where ELLs are welcomed, affirmed, and valued. In addition to presenting the core tenets of this fluidity of diversity model to ELL education, this chapter expanded on how this approach can be applied to instructional strategies and effective learning, while also providing curricular examples.

Key learning theories were presented to make connections to intersectionality and how this, in turn, shapes ELL learning perspectives, growth, and success at varying levels. In adopting a fluid conceptualization of diversity as a framework, an educational commitment is made to promote equity and respect for unique perspectives and their contribution to lifelong learning for ELLs.

REFERENCES

Arce-Trigatti, A., & Silber-Furman, D. (2022). On the way to English proficiency: Language acquisition through culturally relevant pedagogical practice. *NISOD Innovation Abstracts*, *XLIV*(14). Retrieved from nisod.org/2022/09/02/xliv_14/.

Bauer, E. B., Colomer, S. E., & Wiemelt, J. (2018). Biliteracy of African American and Latinx kindergarten students in a dual-language program: Understanding students' translanguaging practices across informal assessments. *Urban Education*, *55*(3), 1–31. https://doi.org/10.1177/0042085918789743

Cloud, N., Genesee, F., & Hamayan, E. (2009). *Literacy instruction for English language learners: A teacher guide to research-based practice.* Heinemann.

Crenshaw, K. (1991). Mapping the margins: Intersectionality, identity politics, and violence against women of color. *Stanford Law Review, 43*(6), 1241–1299.

Cummins, J. (2000). *Language, power and pedagogy: Bilingual children in the crossfire.* Multilingual Matters.

Krashen, S. D. (1987). *Principles and practice in second language acquisition.* Prentice-Hall International.

Krashen, S. D. (2013). *Second language acquisition and use.* Cambridge University Press.

St. Pierre, E. A. (1997). Methodology in the fold and the irruption of transgressive data. *International Journal of Qualitative Studies in Education, 10*(2), 175–189.

WIDA. (2014). *The WIDA English language development standards and resource guide, international edition, KINDERGARTEN–GRADE 12.* Board of Regents of the University of Wisconsin System, on behalf of WIDA.

WIDA. (2020). *Mission Statement.* WIDA University of Wisconsin System. https://wida.wisc.edu/about/mission-history

Chapter 13

Serving English Language Learners with Exceptional and Diverse Needs

Srimani Chakravarthi

As of fall 2015, 14.7% of all ELL students enrolled in public schools, over 713,383 students who were identified and served for English language learner (ELL) needs, were identified with a disability under the Individuals with Disabilities Education Act (National Center for Educational Statistics, 2017). Students who are ELL (henceforth addressed as ELs), served under Section 504 of the Rehabilitation Act (commonly known as the 504 plan), were about 4% of the total population who received 504 accommodations (Civil Rights Data Collection, n.d.).

Note that this total of *over 18%* of identified students with special needs does not include ELs having other diverse needs and who may not be identified. Students with diverse needs within the ELL population remain underserved in most areas, including in identification, assessment, and interventions (U.S. Department of Education, 2004; Park & Thomas, 2012).

It is noted that issues related to educational achievement may often be associated with the second-language acquisition delay rather than disability, which contributes to lack of services that are appropriate and strategically designed to accommodate the diverse need area. This chapter addresses equitable instruction of ELs who have diverse needs, including *identified* special needs.

CASE STUDIES

Case Study #1

Lizbeth is a fifth-grade student at Thigpen elementary. She has been receiving instruction in a bilingual classroom since kindergarten. Her teacher, Mr. Hattie, has been noticing that Lizbeth seems to be preoccupied with several little objects under her desk during class. She is seen playing around with small erasers, toys, and other similar trinkets, which seems to cause her to have less focus on directions in the classroom.

While Mr. Hattie manages to change her seating often in the classroom to have her pair with peers and small groups to complete her work, Lizbeth still manages to bring along trinkets a few times and engages in play activities under the desk. Mr. Hattie has been using proximity control by walking up to her during assigned work to monitor her, which seems to be helping.

Lizbeth also exhibits processing problems, with reading levels more typical of a third grader. Her writing skills seem to be lower as well. Lizbeth can narrate ideas with prompting for essay prompts and can barely write two to three coherent sentences on her own.

Mrs. Acetos, the ELL teacher, pulls Lizbeth out for a half hour each day for small-group instruction in language skills. They also work on their classroom instruction with support in a push-in format, where Mrs. Acetos calls Lizbeth to work in small groups with either her or Mr. Hattie. The small-group setting seems to benefit Lizbeth in focusing and also provides individualized help for writing and reading.

Case Study #2

Danylo is in third grade. He shows excellent language skills and improvement in English, having moved from Ukraine when he was in preschool. However, his teacher notices that he exhibits several delays in language processing that seem unrelated to his second-language acquisition. Although Danylo manages to hold a social conversation with his parents and siblings, he has had no academic instruction in his first language, Ukrainian. Danylo shows excellent behavior in class and attends to instruction, while participating orally and showing adequate auditory comprehension. However, Danylo struggles to summarize his reading and shows delays in writing. His ideas seem to flow faster than his ability to spell and compose sentences. He often forgets what he was thinking as he labors through the written narrative for a given essay prompt.

While teachers who teach in bilingual and ELL settings are trained in evidence-based methods of teaching culturally and linguistically diverse students, challenges such as the ones Lizbeth and Danylo present relate to possible special and other diverse needs. Lizbeth was evaluated for special needs and receives services under a 504 plan, with accommodations of extended time on tests, frequent check-ins, and assignments broken down into smaller steps. However, Danylo did not qualify for any special services after being evaluated for special needs.

PROVISIONS FOR STUDENTS
IDENTIFIED WITH DISABILITIES

Students who exhibit special needs may qualify for special education, which provides them with an Individualized Education Plan (IEP) or a 504 plan that outlines accommodations that facilitate access. The Individuals with Disabilities Act (IDEA) grants provisions for special education services to be provided for all students between 3–21 years who have a disability in one of the 13 categories as identified using the state's recommended criteria for assessment and identification. Students who meet the criteria for the disability identification, as determined by a series of diagnostic assessments, are considered eligible for special education and related services including speech, social work, and other services.

The Office of Civil Rights ensures that students with disabilities are not discriminated against, and this is ensured by providing students with identified disabilities under Section 504 of the Rehabilitation Act with an accommodations plan for the student to enable access. Students who have a 504 plan are typically not seen by a special education teacher and receive their accommodations from the general education teacher, including the ELL teacher. Accommodations under 504 focus on creating equitable access by providing for aspects such as not penalizing for lack of oral participation, providing frequent breaks, utilizing headphones to calm the student, and so on.

However, several issues underlie the identification under IDEA that lead to disproportional over- and underrepresentation of ELs (U.S. Department of Education, 2016). Most of the assessments that are conducted as part of the disability evaluations contain a strong emphasis on language-processing skills, making this a complex process for the linguistically diverse population. In order to address equitable assessment procedures, IDEA has several mandates in place to assure that the linguistic bias is reduced to focus on the disability determination and ensure that the characteristics represented are indicative of an underlying disability.

The U.S. Department of Education (2016) has also put together a useful toolkit to address the unique challenges faced in determination and provision of special services to ELs with disabilities, which includes the steps to the referral process for special education evaluation, mandates for assessment of ELs, and also possible EL characteristics that may interfere with disability determination. This toolkit is available at https://www2.ed.gov/about/offices /list/oela/english-learner-toolkit/chap6.pdf. Tools #2, #3 and #5 in this toolkit are useful sources of information for teachers and practitioners. Below is a brief overview of the contents in the tools, and figure 13.1 provides a sample toolkit.

- *Tool #2: Considering the Influence of Language Difference and Disability on Learning Behaviors* compares characteristics of language differences and disabilities in each of the learning areas: oral comprehension/listening, speaking/oral fluency, phonemic awareness/reading, reading comprehension/vocabulary, writing, spelling, mathematics, handwriting, and behavior.
- *Tool #3: Developing an IEP for an EL with a Disability* includes a checklist for IEP teams to consider, while developing the IEP for the EL with a disability.
- *Tool #5: Selecting Appropriate Accommodations for Students with Disabilities* contains a list of dos and don'ts when selecting classroom and testing accommodations.

Reading Comprehension and Vocabulary

Learning Behavior Manifested	Indicators of a Language Difference due to 2nd Language Acquisition	Indicators of a Possible Learning Disability
Student does not understand passage read, although may be able to read w/ fluency and accuracy	Lacks understanding and background knowledge of topic in L2; is unable to use contextual clues to assist with meaning; improvement seen over time as L2 proficiency increases	Student doesn't remember or comprehend what was read in L1 or L2 (only applicable if student has received instruction in L1); this does not improve over time; this may be due to a memory or processing deficit
Does not understand key words/ phrases; poor comprehension	Lacks understanding of vocabulary and meaning in English	The student's difficulty with comprehension and vocabulary is seen in L1 and L2

Figure 13.1. Sample from the USDOE Toolkit for ELs with Disabilities. *Retrieved from page 8 of "Tools and Resources for Addressing English Learners with Disabilities" in the English Learner Tool Kit. USDOE website at https://www2.ed.gov/about/offices/list/ oela/english-learner-toolkit/chap6.pdf*

In addition, several states have published guidelines for identification, assessment, and intervention of ELs with disabilities to avoid disproportional representation (REL, 2018).

ELL STUDENTS WHO EXHIBIT DIVERSE NEEDS
THAT MAY NOT BE LABELED OR IDENTIFIED

The process of special education referral and evaluation may not always lead to a disability diagnosis or the provision of an IEP or 504 plan, as seen in the case of Danylo earlier in the chapter. This leads to the question of equitable education for those who exhibit problems like Danylo and need more than what the classroom or ELL teacher is able to provide. The primary ways to approach the diverse needs would be to look at the area of needs to make a determination of how best to provide access to materials to eliminate the language or other diverse barriers.

The first and foremost consideration should be instruction that uses the principles of Universal Design for Learning (UDL) to create equitable access to all diverse needs. Studies are emerging to show how UDL-based instruction is effective for ELs with diverse needs (Proctor et al., 2007; Daniel et al., 2014). The three principles of UDL—multiple means to (1) engage, (2) represent, and (3) express (CAST, 2018)—address a variety of EL needs as well as needs due to other cognition, processing, or behavior issues (see figure 13.2).

Key questions to consider while planning	ELL characteristics addressed	Possible diverse needs addressed
Multiple means to Engage: Think about how learners will engage with the lesson.		
Does the lesson provide options that can help all learners? - Regulate their own learning? - Sustain effort and motivation? - Engage and interest all learners?	- Receptive and expressive language may hinder engagement - Cultural component may hinder motivation and interest.	- Difficulty with self-regulation (planning, evaluation, execution) - Difficulty with sustained attention, persistence, motivation - Difficulty with engagement
Multiple means to Represent: Think about how information is presented to learners.		
Does the information provide options that help all learners? - Reach higher levels of comprehension and understanding? - Understand the symbols and expressions? - Perceive what needs to be learned?	- Comprehension affected by language difference - Academic language difficulties - Cultural differences interfering with relating to content - Symbols and expressions are unfamiliar.	- Visual/auditory processing difficulties may hinder comprehension - Difficulties in finding words, key idea due to processing issues. - Difficulty perceiving the order of symbols, words or images - Memory & organization deficits may interfere in making connections in learning.
Multiple means to Express: Think about how learners are expected to act strategically and express themselves		
Does the activity provide options that help all learners? - Act strategically? - Express themselves fluently? - Physically respond?	- Oral expression may be hindered by academic language difficulties - Using response mode that relies on language & communication may hinder expression of content.	- Difficulty with metacognition - Oral language issues (Ex. stuttering, articulation, etc.) - Recall may be inhibited due to inefficient storage and retrieval in long-term memory (organization)

Figure 13.2. UDL Key Questions and ELs Characteristics and Diverse Needs Addressed. *Author created.*

The next consideration would be to accommodate for diverse needs using the characteristics displayed by the learner as the guiding point. The learner can be provided with accommodations (e.g., a calculator, an audio recording of the text) to compensate for slower or weaker prerequisite skills, helping free up cognitive space and moving the learner toward more complex skills such as fractions/decimals and comprehension of text.

Several special education evidence-based practices have been shown to benefit ELs with diverse needs such as explicit and systematic instruction that is scaffolded (Vaughn et al., 2006), peer-assisted learning strategies (Saenz et al., 2005), and teaching foundational reading skills (Nelson et al., 2011). Here are some instructional interventions and accommodations in common areas of difficulties seen in classrooms:

Difficulties in Listening and Speaking

- *Cannot follow oral directions in academic tasks?* Avoid multiple directions; pair with visuals; use slower pace of instruction; delay instructions until step is completed; use peer modeling.
- *Cannot explain process or steps?* Provide sentence frames, visual/word models, word bank.
- *Difficulty with talking due to anxiety; memory or speech difficulties?* Provide alternative ways to express; use private recorded versions to avoid public speaking.
- *Lacks appropriate social communication?* Use role plays; show models of expected behavior; redirect with appropriate social communication use; use positive praise.

Difficulties in Reading

- *Difficulty in sounding out words?* Provide explicit phonological and phonemic instruction.
- *Difficulty decoding words?* Teach word parts; teach morphology of words; use auditory cues; use software like Rewordify to present reading in simple/lower readability levels.
- *Difficulty acquiring and using academic words?* Teach word roots; provide word bank, vocabulary organizers, concept map to show relationship of words, synonyms, antonyms.
- *Difficulty with fluency?* Provide low-readability texts, audio recording of text to listen to before/during reading to allow focusing on meaning-making and making connections.
- *Difficulty in identifying main idea; details in readings?* Activate background knowledge; encourage listening; use modeling; show examples and nonexamples; highlight key information; teach comprehension strategies.

Difficulties in Writing

- *Inability to organize information?* Provide and teach how to use graphic organizers.
- *Cannot recall words?* Provide speech-to-text to help ideas flow, word bank, prediction tools.
- *Spelling/Punctuation difficulties?* Use word processors/prediction tools, grammar/spell-check tools.
- *Cannot write legibly or has motor difficulties?* Use pencil grips, word processor, speech-to-text.

Difficulties in Mathematics

- *Computation difficulties?* Teach with concrete examples; teach prerequisite skills.
- *Problem-solving difficulties?* Teach visualization and problem-solving strategies; provide word bank.
- *Difficulty recalling steps?* Use model solved example, checklist for solving, self-monitoring.

Difficulties in Behavior

- *Cannot stay seated for long?* Use wiggly seats or seat cushions that move; create more movement-based work; provide frequent movement; provide incentive to complete tasks; provide sensory fidgets.
- *Defiant/disruptive?* Create opportunities to lead/excel in class; use preferred activities to motivate.

Difficulties in Executive Functions (Attention, Memory, Organization, Prioritizing, Planning, etc.)

- *Inability to sustain attention/focus?* Use positive behavior supports; call to attention using explicit attention strategies; teach in smaller chunks; use noise-canceling headphones.
- *Inability to recall/retain information?* Use memory strategies; show explicit organization of ideas; teach to fluency; loop skills until maintenance and generalization are achieved.
- *Inability to complete/turn in work?* Use external organizers and reminder tools; break up tasks into manageable smaller chunks; set due dates for smaller chunks.
- *Inability to attend to or fix errors?* Use checklists; teach self-monitoring, self-regulation.

There are also several web-based resources that provide information on interventions for classroom application for a range of learners, some with instructional videos showing classroom practice:

- National Center for Intensive Intervention: https://intensiveintervention.org
- Doing What Works Library: https://dwwlibrary.wested.org
- Center on Positive Behavior Intervention & Supports (PBIS): https://www.pbis.org/topics/classroom-pbis
- Institute of Educational Sciences Practice guides: https://ies.ed.gov/ncee/wwc/PracticeGuides
- California Practitioners Guide for Educating ELs with Disabilities: https://www.cde.ca.gov/sp/se/ac/documents/ab2785guide.pdf

Equitable practices for all ELs with exceptional and other diverse needs can be easy to locate and implement. All this requires is a shift to a social justice perspective, consideration of all areas of disability and diverse classroom-based needs, and use of universal design practices while accommodating to compensate for their specific need areas.

REFERENCES

CAST. (2018). *Universal Design for Learning guidelines version 2.2.* http://udlguidelines.cast.org

Civil Rights Data Collection. (n.d.). *2015–16 English language instruction program enrollment estimations.* Retrieved September 29, 2021, from https://ocrdata.ed.gov/estimations/2015-2016

Daniel, M. C., Shin, D. S., Harrison, C., & Aoki, E. (2014). Examining paths to digital literacies for English language learners. *Illinois Reading Council Journal, 42*(4), 35–42.

National Center for Educational Statistics (2017). *English language learner (ELL) students enrolled in public elementary and secondary schools, by grade, home language and selected student characteristics: Selected years, 2008–09 through fall 2015.* https://nces.ed.gov/programs/digest/d17/tables/dt17_204.27.asp?referer=raceindicators

Nelson, J., Vadasy, P., & Sanders, E. (2011). Efficacy of a tier 2 supplemental root word vocabulary and decoding intervention with kindergarten Spanish speaking English learners. *Journal of Literacy Research, 43*(2), 184–211. doi:10.1177/1086296X11403088

Park, Y., & Thomas, R. (2012). Educating English-language learners with special needs: Cultural and linguistic considerations. *Journal of Education and Practice, 3*(9).

Proctor, P. C., Dalton, B., & Grisham, D. L. (2007). Scaffolding English language learners and struggling readers in a universal literacy environment with embedded strategy instruction and vocabulary support. *Journal of Literacy Research, 39*(1), 71–93.

REL. (2018). *Guidance manuals for educators of English learners with disabilities.* https://ies.ed.gov/ncee/edlabs/regions/west/Ask/Details/68

Saenz, L. M., Fuchs, L. S., & Fuchs, D. (2005). Peer-assisted learning strategies for English language learners with learning disabilities. *Exceptional Children, 71*(3), 231–247.

U.S. Department of Education. (2004). *National symposium on learning disabilities in English language learners.* October 14–15, 2003, Washington, D.C. https://www2.ed.gov/about/offices/list/osers/products/ld-ell/ld-ell.pdf

U.S. Department of Education. (2016). Tools and resources for addressing English learners with disabilities. In *English Learner Tool Kit* (chapter 6). https://www2.ed.gov/about/offices/list/oela/english-learner-toolkit/chap6.pdf

Vaughn, S., Cirino, P. T., Linan-Thompson, S., Mathes, P. G., Carlson, C. D., Hagan, E. C., Pollard-Durodola, S. D., Fletcher, J. M., & Francis, D. J. (2006). Effectiveness of a Spanish intervention and an English intervention for English language learners at risk for reading problems. *American Educational Research Journal, 43*(3), 449–487. doi:10.3102/00028312043003449

Chapter 14

Effective Learning Environments for English Learners

Abbey Bachmann

After years of teaching at a variety of grade levels in Houston, one of the most diverse cities in the nation, experience with English learners (ELs) is something all teachers will gain. One of the most important aspects of helping English learners experience success in the classroom is fostering a learning environment in which all learners feel comfortable. If students feel comfortable and safe in a classroom environment, then they are much more willing to take risks and step outside of their comfort zone. This willingness to try new things can be utilized by educators to help students make great strides in their learning. The following suggestions can help to create an inclusive classroom environment that sets the stage for meaningful learning to take place.

GET TO KNOW EL STUDENTS AND THE THINGS THEY LOVE

In the United States, ELs often feel like they are the outsiders in the classroom. Occasionally, there are other students who speak their first language, but this is not always the case. Striving to get to know ELs regardless of an ability to speak their native language is the foundation of an inclusive and welcoming classroom.

What hobbies do they enjoy? What are their favorite subjects? What sort of music do they listen to? Do they have any siblings? Before any unit is implemented in the classroom, regardless of content area, teachers should take a student-interest inventory in order to effectively use materials and texts that are connected and related to student interests. For example, as an

English teacher, selecting texts for an informational text unit that deals with common student interests will create greater buy-in from the start of the lesson. Students will be interested in the material, but they will also be aware that their teacher took notice of their interests in order to provide them with materials that are engaging.

When possible, providing students with a choice of texts or classroom topics is ideal. When students are provided with the opportunity to choose a text, topic, or material that interests them, they are going to have more self-efficacy, intrinsic motivation, and autonomy (Allred & Cena, 2020). Free-choice reading units allow students to select a text of their choice in order to read in class and apply the skills being taught. Student choice can be utilized in all classrooms regardless of the content. In history courses, if students are learning about a particular war or battle, they could be provided with a variety of texts to read about the same topic. Some texts may be written during different time periods, written by different authors, or presented in different formats.

When planning lessons, build in content that appeals to students' interests. If teaching literature circles, select texts that appeal to students. If selecting nonfiction texts for a lesson, include choices that students will find interesting. Once students catch on that you listen to them and that you have tried to appeal to their interests, they are much more willing to complete the work that you ask of them. If students are going to be asked to complete work that is academically demanding, that should be the only hurdle in front of them. They should not have to struggle through a topic they are not engaged with in addition to figuring out what the words themselves mean.

LET THEM GET TO KNOW YOU

Share just enough personal information about yourself with your students in order to appear human to them. So often students think that teachers only exist within the confines of their classroom; however, when teachers share a little bit about their lives with their students, students are much more willing to complete the work and try hard.

For example, if you as a teacher are currently a graduate student earning an additional degree or certification, share that you understand what students are going through with school: for example, trying to balance coursework, study, have jobs outside the classroom, and enjoy time with friends. Hopefully, they will understand that your life is busy too, and they will realize that you are still there for them every day.

Always put 100% into your teaching even when you may have a million other things on your plate. From experience, it seems that English learners rise to the challenge. No longer are you just a teacher who doesn't understand them and is trying to make their lives difficult; you are a person who is there for them, helping them because you care despite what is on your personal plate.

Include a little bit of yourself and your personality in the content you present to your students. Sometimes it's as simple as a Bitmoji that is included on lesson slides. Occasionally, you may choose to use yourself, your family, or your interests to present materials and lessons to students. When writing sample sentences or scenarios to demonstrate a concept or skills, make those sentences about you or your hobbies. For example, when teaching compound sentences, use a sentence such as "My dog is a yellow lab, and her name is Ella" instead of a generic sentence from a grammar workbook. A picture of your dog could even be included as part of this example. This allows the opportunity for teachers to make a personal connection with their students while still teaching the required content.

If you are lucky enough to be able to teach in the same classroom all day, using the physical space of your classroom as a means to communicate with your students about you is effective as well. Personal pictures and mementos from home allow students a glimpse into who you are as an individual. Students will notice and seek out information about your objects and pictures, which can lead to many opportunities for connection.

Showing students that you make mistakes and sometimes struggle is an important aspect of showing them a little bit of who you are. So often, students see the academic expectations that teachers have for them as unobtainable. However, if teachers can model the learning process for students, mistakes and all, students will feel more confident in trying to complete more difficult and rigorous tasks.

Whenever students are asked to complete a writing assignment, modeling an example for your students is key. You should not aim to show students a product that you completed the night before, but write it with them. Show them the struggles and mistakes that you may make in the process. This helps them to understand that struggling and making mistakes is acceptable. Their work will not always be perfect the first time they complete it, but if teachers only show pristine, completed products, students will not learn the importance of academic struggle.

SHOW YOUR EL STUDENTS THAT YOU CARE

Ask them what will help them be successful. Give them time to process, but also make sure they feel comfortable asking you questions. Unfortunately, many ELs slip through the cracks in schools.

For example, a former student, currently an 11th-grade English learner, is my mentee at the school where I currently work. This means I monitor his grades and work with him to ensure he is successful. When I see failing grades in his classes, I often approach teachers to ask what I can do to help him be successful in their class. The most typical response is that he doesn't ask questions, that he's too quiet. It becomes a difficult conversation to have with some teachers to explain that it is best practice for the teacher to check with him as to whether or not he understands the material or has questions. He may not feel comfortable or confident enough to raise his hand and ask you, but you should anticipate questions from him and not make it uncomfortable for him to do so.

EL students have to feel comfortable in a classroom environment in order to ask questions. Asking questions and admitting that they do not understand a concept makes them vulnerable. Instinctually, this is something all humans avoid feeling. We want to be confident and competent, and our EL students are no exception. Being approachable and understanding as a teacher allows EL students to feel more comfortable and confident in letting you know when they do not understand a concept or lesson.

Go to their events/games. Taking interest in what your students excel at outside of the classroom will communicate your investment in who they are as an individual. If we want students to let us into their lives in order to make connections with them, we need to communicate that we care about them outside of our classrooms. The easiest way to do this is to make appearances at their extracurricular events.

Whether it is a soccer game, orchestra concert, or art show, make time to show up, even if just for a little while. If students do not see you at the event, make sure you let them know that you enjoyed their performance when in class the next day. While they may not openly let you see their excitement, they will no doubt remember that you supported them in the events that matter the most to them.

Give them the opportunity to share with you. Creating your class assignments and activities with students in mind is crucial. Build in moments for students to share their lives and what's on their mind with you. Whether through journaling, exit tickets, warm-up responses, or reflections, small time built into lessons for connections can add up to make a big difference. In English courses, students are often asked to make connections to the text they are reading. How are the ideas presented in the text relevant to their lives or the world in which they live? If EL students feel their voice matters, teachers are bound to hear their voices a lot more often.

PRAISE THEIR EFFORTS

Often, English learners want nothing more than to blend in with their peers. When they ask questions, get a good grade on an assignment, and show engagement in class, praise that effort. A positive reward ticket system is something that has been used in classrooms that really helps some of the most introverted students flourish.

Passing out tickets for answering questions, being prepared in class, and following directions is an immediate positive behavior reinforcement. These tickets can be used for snacks, candy, and grade incentives such as homework passes. Even the most shy students will put forth more of an effort when these efforts are being praised.

Positive phone calls home are a rewarding and valuable positive reinforcement tool, especially for families who may not hear from schools or teachers for positive reasons on a regular basis. Parents of English learners often receive communication from schools in English and occasionally in Spanish as well, but communication from the teacher often comes in English exclusively.

Using Google Translate to send home a positive email to parents regarding their students can show the parents and student alike that you really have noticed their efforts and appreciate having the student in your class. Google Translate may make a few errors, but parents will get a better understanding of what you are trying to say rather than relying exclusively on using English. If you have a coworker who speaks the child's native language and they are willing to help you make a phone call, this is also a great option to reach out to the families of English learners.

Comments and feedback left on student papers and assignments can go a long way to make connections and build relationships with English learners. When a student has completed an assignment correctly, given an insightful response, or shown progress in their academic work quality, indicate your approval with comments such as "good work!" or "nice job" or "great progress" on their papers. Stickers are still a prized reward for adolescents, despite their constant desire to move beyond some "childish" items in their lives.

Positive feedback can also be directed toward English learners orally as well. If you call on a student who gives you a correct or satisfactory answer, make sure you acknowledge their effort and their response. For English learners, cold-calling may not be the most ideal way to assess their understanding. Allowing these students to volunteer to share an answer or calling on them if you know for certain that they have the correct answer can help to build confidence and trust in the student rather than resentment.

Building relationships and establishing a warm, inviting classroom environment are the most important aspects of helping English learners achieve success in the classroom. Teachers can be masters of their content area, but if there is no relationship on which the content stands, all the effort spent teaching the content is in vain. These relationships are extremely important for learners who need the encouragement, support, and motivation to achieve success in the classroom.

REFERENCES

Allred, J. B., & Cena, M. E. (2020). Reading motivation in high school: Instructional shifts in student choice and class time. *Journal of Adolescent & Adult Literacy, 64*(1), 27–35.

Chapter 15

Culturally Responsive Social-Emotional Learning for ELL Students with Limited or Interrupted Formal Education

Jessica Furrer and Sara Castro-Olivo

Javier and Barbara sat next to each other as two of 19 students in a ninth-grade English as a Second Language (ESL) classroom. This classroom was housed in a highly diverse school in Texas where over 50% of the student population was receiving services for English Language Development (ELD). Students in this class came from various parts of the world (e.g., Mexico, Honduras, El Salvador, Syria, China, Philippines).

The majority were Spanish speakers and had only lived in the United States for 2 years or less. Javier and Barbara stood out from the rest of the group. First of all, they were older than the rest. Javier was 19 and Barbara, 17. Although they were older, they were equally youthful in their energy as the rest of their peers. They playfully tried out pronouncing English words, and they seemed excited to be in school, like every teacher loves to see.

Within a few days, Javier and Barbara continued to stand out, but now it was for being confused in class, even after a classmate would translate the word *synonym* to them in Spanish; it wasn't a term they knew (e.g., *contemporary = contemporaneo*). Peers would verbally spell words for them while they wrote so they did not need to look back and forth at the board, but Javier would switch *b* for *d* and then get instructed on how to form the letters. His frustration grew quickly as he started to notice how far behind his academic skills were when compared to his peers. Barbara would also express frustration and shame for not being able to do the work she was being presented with.

By the end of the year, Javier and Barbara were writing some sentences using stems, while their peers were writing essays. Both students and the teacher, admittedly, were overwhelmed seeing the huge gaps compared to their peers. Javier and Barbara started to put their heads down whenever presented with grade-level academic work. Javier became more withdrawn and serious; he would often ask his teacher, "Why come to school? I can't do it. I could make money working instead." By the following year, Javier had dropped out to work, and Barbara had to repeat ninth grade, now as an 18-year-old.

Students like Javier and Barbara are the focus of this chapter. Although Javier and Barbara were very different in many ways, they had something in common. They were both students with limited or interrupted formal education (SLIFE). In this chapter, we define the SLIFE population, summarize their diverse academic and social-emotional needs, and discuss some of their multiple strengths that can easily facilitate their academic and social-emotional resilience. In addition, we describe best practices for social-emotional learning (SEL) program planning and delivery for English language learners (ELLs) and SLIFE, sample triage/benchmarking, and ways educators can employ a multi-tiered level of support systems for SLIFE.

HETEROGENEITY OF ELLS

Most school districts tend to place all ELLs in the same classroom and programming based on age, scores on English language-proficiency tests, and grade level; however, they often neglect to realize that not all ELLs have had the same experiences or needs. For most ELL students, their needs go beyond English language acquisition. Some ELLs may be U.S.-born or foreign-born and, as a result, have different educational experiences, outcomes, and needs. For example, foreign-born Hispanic students have four times the dropout rate of U.S.-born Hispanics (Laird et al., 2007). Foreign-born ELLs could be diplomat immigrants, children of migrant farm workers, or refugees with unique educational backgrounds and/or documentation status. The United Nations Children's Fund (2018) has noted nearly a 50% increase in immigration, resulting in an estimated 30 million immigrant children in the past 20 years.

Take one high school ESL classroom of 19 students as an example. One student from Mexico may have been from a large city where they attended school and after-school academic activities 5 days a week, comparable to the U.S. public education system. Another student sitting nearby may also be from Mexico, but from a rural area in southern Mexico where everyone spoke one of the 96 different indigenous languages spoken in Mexico and had little access to formal education.

A student across the room from El Salvador may have attended school initially in first and second grade but had to leave in favor of working to financially support their family, like Javier. An additional student sitting in the front may be from Syria, where they halted school attendance for years due to an increasingly unsafe environment, before attending school in an asylum country and ultimately resettling in the United States. All of these students could be identified as SLIFE and be placed in the same ESL class as those students who are long-term ELLs and have received formal continuous instruction since kindergarten.

SLIFE POPULATION BACKGROUND

SLIFE are students who, for a variety of reasons, have missed substantial amounts (i.e., usually more than 2 years) of formal schooling and, by U.S. educational standards, are academically behind compared to same-age or same-grade peers. They may be behind a couple years in content knowledge in all academic subjects or, like Javier and Barbara, have emerging literacy skills. They may also have unique social-emotional or behavioral needs (DeCapua & Marshall, 2011).

It is estimated that more than 1 in 10 ELLs are SLIFE and 60% of SLIFE are high school age (Potochnick, 2018). However, these statistics may under-report SLIFE, as the U.S. Department of Education is not currently collecting data on the number of SLIFE students enrolled in our public school system. Different states and districts vary in who, and how, they identify their SLIFE population—if they do it at all. One high school ESL teacher in a district that tracks SLIFE makes the distinction of district identified vs. unidentified SLIFE given her experience with a number of students without initial district identification but who were discovered to have limited academic skills in their first language through classroom instruction.

SLIFE are also challenging to identify due to the variation of academic skill they experience. The Bridges to Academic Success program serves SLIFE adolescents and delineates a distinct subpopulation of SLIFE called SLIFE with Developing Literacy (SDL; Auslander, 2019). Compared to SLIFE, SDL are new to reading or have reading skills below a third-grade level in their home language, and therefore have distinct needs from SLIFE who might be enrolled in high school but with a seventh-grade reading level. Given that most districts are not yet at a place of tracking SDL, SLIFE as a whole are the focus of this chapter.

UNIQUE ACADEMIC, SOCIAL, AND
EMOTIONAL NEEDS OF SLIFE

SLIFE have been identified as having greater risk of academic failure and dropping out compared to other foreign-born ELLs who have attended school continuously (Potochnik, 2018; Fry, 2005). They also have a greater risk of being pushed out by aging out of the system. SLIFE's ages do not always align with previous educational experience or grade placement. For example, a 17-year-old who reports completing school until sixth grade may be placed not in a grade matching their age but in ninth grade and will need to pass the appropriate classes and district/state exams to advance and graduate. However, students and their teachers are racing against the clock to catch SLIFE up to their same-grade peers before they are too old to continue traditional high school.

Many teachers report their uncertainty in how to bridge these academic knowledge gaps in a relatively short time period. They report a lack of educational resources that (1) meet students at their current level of performance and (2) are developmentally appropriate. For example, teachers and SLIFE have to choose between either (1) leveled readers that are too text heavy but are more developmentally engaging or (2) readers with appropriate difficulty level of text that have topics that are not of interest to adolescents and may include images of young children, not adolescents who look like them. Although academic skill gaps, academic resource gaps, and systemic barriers such as aging out are evident challenges for SLIFE, SLIFE have relevant social and emotional needs to note.

Both foreign-born students and SLIFE have experienced immigration. For refugees or immigrants, the main reason to move to the United States may have been due to war or community violence, persecution, or economic hardship. Undocumented immigrants may face dangerous journeys to the United States, detainment in detention facilities, or long separations from parental figures. They may experience grief following the loss of important people and places following arrival.

Foreign-born ELLs also experience acculturative stress, which has been described as the stress felt from being exposed to a new culture (i.e., new languages, social and behavior expectations, discrimination, and values and norms; Liebkind & Jesinskaja-Lahti, 2000). High levels of acculturative stress have been found to be associated with depression and anxiety (Constantine et al., 2004) and lower academic performance (Albeg & Castro-Olivo, 2014) and aspirations (Widales-Benitez et al., 2017). One could expect SLIFE to be at increased risk for stress beyond that of a typical foreign-born ELL, as it may have been years since they last attended school prior to their arrival in the United States, and this makes them feel out of place even with other ELL peers, which will have a negative effect in their relationships as well.

SLIFE may be unfamiliar with basic classroom rules/norms. For example, they may be unfamiliar with raising their hand to ask a question, or that handouts are usually completed independently without teacher or peer support, or even writing their name on the top of the paper. The first author of this chapter interviewed an ESL teacher a few years ago who indicated that in her experience, many SLIFE had difficulty with organization, arriving on time to class and prepared with materials, and sitting in their assigned seats.

She also noted that their absence from formal school culture negatively impacts socialization of school rules and behavior norms, including how to effectively communicate with peers and teachers. They may feel particularly isolated or socially outcast when comparing themselves to other ELLs due to their academic achievement, the books they are reading, difficulty adjusting to classroom procedures, or difficulty developing social skills in the school context.

Students who are socially outcast have been found to have decreased self-esteem, sense of school belonging, and ethnic pride (Gordon, 1996). There is also an increase of stress, anger, and interpersonal conflicts when students are socially outcast (Suárez-Orozco & Suárez-Orozco, 2001). Although schools are the primary place of socialization as a student, schools have been found to not necessarily represent a safe space for ELLs (Martinez et al., 2004). For example, Martinez et al. (2004) found that ELLs often report being victimized/bullied in the classrooms and often feel unprepared to get help.

SOCIAL-EMOTIONAL LEARNING FOR SLIFE

Social-emotional learning programs have gained considerable popularity in the last 2 decades. SEL is defined as the skills needed in order to live a productive and satisfying life within our global society (Collaborative for Academic, Social, and Emotional Learning, 2020). SEL has been effectively taught in school settings and improves students' social-emotional and academic outcomes (Taylor et al., 2017). SEL usually teaches students five core competencies.

Those competencies are: (1) self-awareness, (2) social awareness, (3) self-management, (4) responsible decision-making, and (5) relationship skills. Table 15.1 suggests how we see each of the five SEL competencies being used to support the social-emotional and academic needs of SLIFE.

SEL programs build skills in weak areas, but they also can utilize the students' strengths. Some research notes that SLIFE are particularly determined to graduate, they have high academic engagement and high academic

**Table 15.1. Sample SEL Competencies for SLIFE's Academic and
Social-Emotional Outcomes**

SEL Competency	Academic Skills	Social-Emotional Learning
Self-Awareness	Learn to identify academic skills that are above their current level of performance Learn to identify when frustration is due to lack of academic fluency	Learn to identify when lack of academic skills makes them feel down/upset
Social Awareness	Learn to identify peers who are willing to help with academic skills Learn ways to ask for help	Learn to empathize with parents and cope with familial acculturation gaps. Learn how identify and ignore microaggressions.
Responsible Decision-Making	Learn to identify short- and long-term goals to make progress in academic areas and English language	Learn to identify peers who help them stay on track with goals
Relationship Skills	Learn how to initiate peer academic support groups Learn to ask teachers for help in a prosocial manner	Learn how to initiate positive relationships with teachers and peers in the classroom setting
Self- Management	Learn to raise their hand when they need help or ask for pre-teaching opportunities for topics they already know are difficult for them.	Learn to use cognitive restructuring skills to cope with acculturative stress and perceived discrimination

aspirations, they demonstrate openness to trying new things, they value social connection and support, and they demonstrate strong support-seeking behavior (Bang & Collet, 2018; Porter, 2013). This engagement and motivation, often labeled as the immigrant paradox, may protect SLIFE from dropout, but for how long? For Javier, it seemed to last about a year. How do we foster these strengths so SLIFE persist through the difficulties mentioned above?

Research on SLIFE and SEL is at its infancy stage; however, teachers can use lessons learned from previous research on culturally responsive teaching to identify the adaptations needed to make SEL instruction effective at meeting the needs of their SLIFE. DeCapua and Marshall (2011) explored culturally responsive instruction for SLIFE and have shown the importance of making all instruction relevant and relatable to students.

They also recommend considering SLIFE cultural realities and strengths, such as their oral language skills, real-world experiences, and values of community. Castro-Olivo (2010) argued that SEL programs also need to be culturally responsive by first keeping the unique risk and protective factors of ELLs in mind. Castro-Olivo has shown in multiple studies that cultural adaptations to SEL programs are feasible for school settings and produce positive outcomes for students (Castro-Olivo, 2014; Castro-Olivo & Merrell; 2012; Castro-Olivo et al., 2016).

What preimmigration, immigration, and post-migration factors have they experienced? For example, if they frequently migrate, perhaps they may be less engaged in building relationships, or putting forth effort in class given how frequently they change schools. This awareness of students' life experiences will inform teachers whether the students will find the beliefs, values, and skills useful and relevant to their cultural reality. The following section provides the readers with the framework Castro-Olivo and her research team have employed to make SEL programs responsive to the needs of ELLs. These frameworks can easily be applied to SLIFE.

BEST PRACTICES FOR SEL PROGRAM PLANNING AND DELIVERY

Since the early 1990s, researchers working with culturally and linguistically diverse populations have identified the need to make adaptations to manualized evidence-based treatments in order to ensure these treatments are effective and well accepted by their target population. One of the most widely used frameworks for cultural adaptations of evidence-based treatments is the Ecology Validity Model (EVM) by Guillermo Bernal and colleagues (1995). Although this framework is over 25 years old, it makes it easy for practitioners to conceptualize that a cultural adaptation is not just about translating the program or having an aide sitting next to target students, trying to have them understand the program as the rest of the class moves on and is fully engaged in the discussions and activities.

The EVM model pushes practitioners to modify programs, like the SEL programs delivered in schools, by attending to the students' *language*, providing them with *interventionists* who are bilingual/bicultural (i.e., culturally competent), using *examples*, *content*, and *context* that is relevant to the risk and protective factors of the target population and is *delivered* in a way that will be acceptable and accessible to the students, and promoting *goals* that are aligned with the goals and values of the target population.

This framework has been applied in school, community, and clinical settings (Peterson et al., 2017). Teachers and school-based mental health care providers working with SLIFE students are urged to adapt their SEL program to ensure all of the eight dimensions previously discussed are carefully adapted to truly meet the unique needs of SLIFE students.

As previously mentioned, research on culturally responsive SEL for SLIFE has yet to be launched. To this date, only one researcher has conducted comprehensive adaptations of evidence-based SEL programs for use with immigrant ELL adolescents (Brown et al., 2018). In 2012, Castro-Olivo and Merrell published an article summarizing the procedures followed to adapt the *Jovenes Fuertes* SEL program.

This program is an adaptation of the *Strong Teens* program and was designed to be implemented with newcomer Hispanic ELL students. The program followed all the lessons and goals of the *Strong Teens* program, but focused on using the SEL skills taught in each lesson to discuss experiences unique to immigrants, such as ethnic identity, perceived discrimination, familial acculturation gaps, and acculturation stress. The *Jovenes Fuertes* program has been tested in school settings multiple times, and each study has shown that students value the adaptations made, report increases on SEL knowledge and resiliency, and learn to cope with sociocultural stressors due to being a part of the program (Castro-Olivo, 2014; Cramer & Castro-Olivo, 2015; Castro-Olivo et al., 2014).

Teachers are encouraged to follow steps similar to those Castro-Olivo and Merrell (2012) followed to adapt *Jovenes Fuertes*, as they adapt any evidence-based SEL school-based program. In addition, school administrators and teachers are also encouraged to employ a systematic screening process to better determine which of their ELL students are SLIFE and in need of additional culturally responsive SEL supports.

Some students are likely to benefit from universal SEL programming as long as it is in a language they can understand and does not rely heavily on written expression; however, students who have experienced higher levels of trauma or acculturative stress should be referred to targeted group or individual counseling support guided by a mental health care professional who can be more attentive to the psycho-social and cultural needs of SLIFE at higher risk. The Coping with Acculturative Stress in American Schools Scale (CASAS; Castro-Olivo et al., 2014) can be used to identify students with higher levels of acculturative stress.

Mental health care providers can use this data to group students and further assess coping styles and/or other mental health problems. In addition, schools should also screen SLIFE for trauma. The Child and Adolescent Trauma Screener by Sachser et al. (2017) has been identified as a valid, reliable, and practical tool for use in school settings (Eklund et al., 2018).

The main goal of all educators is to keep every student engaged in school until graduation. More than just graduating, they want their students' education to be transformational in that it helps them grow into high-achieving, responsible, mature, and passionate adults. Students with limited or interrupted formal education (SLIFE), like Javier and Barbara, are not yet having this experience in school. While Javier and Barbara needed academic interventions to build their academic skills in a short amount of time, they also would have likely benefited from social and emotional supports to be resilient in overcoming sociocultural hurdles and reaching their full potential.

SEL interventions need to be culturally adapted to meet the unique needs of SLIFE by considering factors that are parts of their cultural reality, such as acculturation stress, potential discrimination or social exclusion, and the added effects that limited or interrupted schooling can have on students' social-emotional and academic competencies. We strongly urge every educator who has the privilege of serving SLIFE students to first work with a multidisciplinary team to identify the social-emotional and sociocultural needs of these students. After identifying their needs, the SEL competencies students will gain through these services can be used as stepping stones to academic intervention and success.

REFERENCES

Albeg, L. J., & Castro-Olivo, S. M. (2014). The relationship between mental health, acculturative stress, and academic performance in a Latino middle school sample. *Contemporary School Psychology, 18*(3), 178–186.

Auslander, L. (2019). *Creating responsive classroom communities: A cross-case study of schools serving students with interrupted schooling.* Rowman & Littlefield.

Bang, H., & Collet, B. A. (2018). Educational gaps and their impact on Iraqi refugee students' secondary schooling in the Greater Detroit, Michigan area. *Comparative & International Education, 13*(2), 229–318.

Bernal, G., Bonilla, J., & Bellido, C. (1995). Ecological validity and cultural sensitivity for outcome research: Issues for the cultural adaptation and development of psychosocial treatments with Hispanics. *Journal of Abnormal Child Psychology, 23*(1), 67–82.

Brown, C., Maggin, D. M., & Burren, M. (2018). Systematic review of cultural adaptations of school-based social, emotional, and behavioral interventions for students of color. *Education and Treatment of Children, 41*(4), 431–456.

Castro-Olivo, S. (2010). One size does not fit all: Adapting SEL programs for use in our multicultural world. In K. W. Merrell & B. A. Gueldner (Eds.), *Social and emotional learning in the classroom: Promoting mental health and academic success* (pp. 83–102). Guilford Press.

Castro-Olivo, S. M. (2014). Promoting social-emotional learning in adolescent Latino ELLs: A study of the culturally adapted Strong Teens program. *School Psychology Quarterly, 29*(4), 567.

Castro-Olivo, S., Cramer, K., & Garcia, N. (2016). Manualized school-based intervention curricula for ethnic minority populations. In S. L. Graves & J. Blake (Eds.), *Psychoeducational assessment and intervention for ethnic minority children: Evidence-based approaches.* APA Publications.

Castro-Olivo, S., & Merrell, K. (2012). Validating cultural adaptations of a school-based social-emotional learning programme for use with Latino immigrant adolescents. *Advances in School Mental Health Promotion, 5*(2), 78–92.

Castro-Olivo, S. M., Palardy, G. J., Albeg, L., & Williamson, A. A. (2014). Development and validation of the coping with acculturative stress in American schools (CASAS-A) scale on a Latino adolescent sample. *Assessment for Effective Intervention, 40*(1).

Collaborative for Academic, Social, and Emotional Learning (CASEL). (2020, October 1). *CASEL's SEL framework.* https://casel.org/casel-sel-framework-11 -2020

Constantine, M. G., Okazaki, S., & Utsey, S. O. (2004). Self-concealment, social self-efficacy, acculturative stress, and depression in African, Asian, and Latin American international college students. *American Journal of Orthopsychiatry, 74*(3), 230–241.

Cramer, K. M., & Castro-Olivo, S. (2015). Effects of a culturally adapted social-emotional learning intervention program on students' mental health. *Contemporary School Psychology, 20*(2), 118–129.

DeCapua, A., & Marshall, H. (2011). Reaching ELLs at risk: Instruction for students with limited or interrupted formal education. *Prevention School Failure, 55*(1), 35–41.

Eklund, K., Rossen, E., Koriakin, T., Chafouleas, S. M., & Resnick, C. (2018). A systematic review of trauma screening measures for children and adolescents. *School Psychology Quarterly, 33*(1), 30.

Fry, R. (2005). *The higher dropout rate of foreign-born teens: The role of schooling abroad.* Pew Hispanic Center.

Gordon, K. A. (1996). Resilient Hispanic youths' self-concept and motivational patterns. *Hispanic Journal of Behavioral Sciences, 18*(1), 63–73.

Laird, J., Kienzl, G., DeBell, M., & Chapman, C. (2007). *Dropout rates in the United States: 2005.* Compendium Report, NCES 2007–059. National Center for Education Statistics.

Liebkind, K., & Jasinskaja-Lahti, I. (2000). The influence of experiences of discrimination on psychological stress: A comparison of seven immigrant groups. *Journal of Community and Applied Social Psychology, 10*(1), 1–16.

Martinez Jr, C. R., DeGarmo, D. S., & Eddy, J. M. (2004). Promoting academic success among Latino youths. *Hispanic Journal of Behavioral Sciences, 26*(2), 128–151.

Peterson, L. S., Villarreal, V., & Castro, M. J. (2017). Models and frameworks for culturally responsive adaptations of interventions. *Contemporary School Psychology, 21*(3), 181–190.

Porter, C. (2013). *Honoring counterstories: Utilizing digital storytelling in the culturally responsive classroom to investigate the community cultural wealth and resiliency of students with limited or interrupted formal education (SLIFE)* [Doctoral dissertation]. University of Massachusetts at Boston. ProQuest LLC.

Potochnick, S. (2018). The academic adaptation of immigrant students with interrupted schooling. *American Educational Research Journal, 44*(4), 859–892.

Sachser, C., Berliner, L., Holt, T., Jensen, T. K., Jungbluth, N., Risch, E., Rosner, R., & Goldbeck, L. (2017). International development and psychometric properties of the Child and Adolescent Trauma Screen (CATS). *Journal of Affective Disorders, 210*, 189–195.

Suárez-Orozco, C., & Suárez-Orozco, M. M. (2001). *Children of immigration.* Harvard University Press.

Taylor, R. D., Oberle, E., Durlak, J. A., & Weissburg, R. P. (2017). Promoting positive youth development through school-based social-emotional learning interventions: A meta-analysis of follow-up effects. *Child Development, 88*(4), 1156–1171.

United Nations Children's Fund. (2018). Department of Economic and Social Affairs, Population Division: Trends in international migrant stock: The 2018 revision, migrants by age and sex. https://www.un.org/development/desa/pd/content/international-migrant-stock

Widales-Benitez, O., d'Abreu, A., & Castro-Olivo, S. (August, 2017). The effects of acculturative stress on Latino ELL students' academic aspirations [Poster presentation]. Annual Convention of the American Psychological Association, Washington, DC.

Index

Universal Design for Learning
(UDL), 113
UN Refugee Agency, 92
The Upside Down Boy (Herrera &
Gómez), 66, 67
U.S. Department of Education
toolkit, 111–12

Valenzuela, Angela, 48
Van Buren, Amy, 27–35
VandenBroeck, F., 68, 69
Villegas, A., 10
visual support for students, 13

Wagner-Romero, Jancarlos J., xi–xiv
Walqui, A., 10
Watson, S. M., 31

Watts, J., 65, 68
white, male authors, 56–57
Whorf, B. L., 4
WIDA. *See* World-Class Instructional
Design and Assessment
Wimmer, S., 70–71
World-Class Instructional Design and
Assessment (WIDA), 92, 101–2
worldviews, 76
Wright, W., 95
writing difficulties, 115

Yokota, J., 40
Yoo, Monica S., 9–16
Yum, H., 65, 68

Zhang, A., 68–69

About the Editors

Ashraf Esmail, PhD, is an associate professor and program coordinator of criminal justice at Dillard University. He is the director for the Center for Racial Justice and Barron Hilton Criminal Justice Endowed Professor. His areas of research include race and social justice, multicultural, urban, and peace education. He is on the boards for the National Association for Multicultural Education, National Association for Peace Education, World Association for Academic Doctors, and Court Watch Nola.

Abul Pitre, PhD, is professor and department chair of Africana Studies at San Francisco State University. He was appointed Edinboro University's first named professor for his outstanding work in African American education and held the distinguished title of Carter G. Woodson Professor of Education.

Alice Duhon Ross, PhD, is a core faculty for the Richard W. Riley College of Education at Walden University. Her current research focus is multicultural, international, peace education. She is a career educator with over 30 years of teaching in higher education and is a Nationally Board-Certified Counselor and National Board-Certified School Counselor. She is the past Region 5 Regional Director for the National Association for Multicultural Education Advancing and Avocation for Social Justice & Equity and serves on several advisory and editorial boards.

Judith Blakely, EdD, is an educational specialist. She is certified in multiple states as a school superintendent, school administrator (PK–12 principal), and director of special, bilingual, and gifted education. She is also a member of the National Association for Bilingual Education (providing work and service to the discipline of world language). Dr. Blakely presently serves as academic coordinator at Walden University and works to serve a vital role in maximizing student achievement by incorporating leadership, advocacy, and collaboration. She believes in team effort and works tirelessly to promote equity and access to opportunities and rigorous educational experiences for all students. Her motto is: "Together we can!" Raised in Chicago by her mother and father, a Chicago Public School teacher and a small business owner respectively, Dr. Blakely developed a passion early for education and service. To this end, she co-founded an educational social service agency that advocates for under-represented members of society through personal development, education, and social service programs. With offerings such as advocacy for the special needs community, tutoring, resume writing, goal-setting workshops, parenting workshops, literacy training, student workshops, and teacher classroom assistance, Dr. Blakely empowers individuals and communities to break the cycle of underachievement and create legacies of success. She believes that education is the door to opportunity and living a life of abundance, and that this is a gift that should be afforded to all.

H. Prentice Baptiste, EdD, is a Regents and Distinguished Achievement Professor, and in 2014 was awarded the first College of Education, Diversity Award at New Mexico State University. He was president (2016 to 2018) of the National Association for Multicultural Education (NAME), a premier organization advocating for equity and social justice, which he helped found in 1990. His research interests include the conceptualization of multicultural education, the process of multiculturalizing educational entities, and culturally diversifying science and mathematics instruction. Dr. Baptiste has authored or edited seven books, as well as over 140 articles, papers, and chapters on multicultural and science education He has presented papers and conducted workshops in Nigeria, Egypt, Germany, Jamaica, Kenya, Morocco, and the Netherlands. As president of NAME, he was co-leader of two educational cultural groups to Cuba.

About the Contributors

Andrea Arce-Trigatti, PhD, is an interdisciplinary scholar and faculty member in the Department of Curriculum and Instruction at Tennessee Technological University (TTU).

Abbey Bachmann has been teaching English/language arts in the Houston, Texas, area for the past 11 years.

Sara Castro-Olivo, PhD, NCSP, is an associate professor in the school psychology program at Texas A&M University.

Srimani Chakravarthi, PhD, is a professor of education at the University of St. Francis in Joliet, Illinois.

Amina Chaudhri, PhD, is an associate professor in the Teacher Education Department at Northeastern Illinois University.

James Cohen, PhD, is an associate professor of ESL/bilingual education in the Department of Curriculum and Instruction at Northern Illinois University.

Daniela DiGregorio, PhD, works as an assistant professor of education and TESOL at Wilson College, Pennsylvania.

Lisa Fetman, PhD, is a researcher and lecturer in the Department of Teaching and Learning at the University of Colorado, Colorado Springs, and an adjunct professor in the educational leadership program at Florida Southern College.

Jessica Furrer, MEd, is a doctoral student in the school psychology program at Texas A&M University.

Esther Garza, PhD, is an associate professor of bilingual & ESL education at Texas A&M University–San Antonio.

Veronica Garza, EdD, is a researcher in the Department of Teaching and Learning at the University of Colorado, Colorado Springs, and a lecturer for graduate education courses in San Diego.

Leslie Grant, PhD, is an associate professor in TESOL (Teaching English to Speakers of Other Languages) in the Department of Teaching and Learning at the University of Colorado, Colorado Springs.

Magdalena Haro is an elementary education major earning the bilingual endorsement from the Department of Curriculum and Instruction at Northern Illinois University.

Sarah Heinz is an elementary education major earning the ESL endorsement from the Department of Curriculum and Instruction at Northern Illinois University.

Jesslyn Hollar, PhD, is the founder and director of Edology Consulting, LLC.

Jim Hollar, PhD, is a faculty member and coordinator for secondary education and the Accelerated Secondary Program (ASP) at Edgewood College in Madison, Wisconsin.

SoYoung Kang, PhD, is currently an adjunct professor of education at Gwynedd Mercy University in Pennsylvania.

Mariola Krol, EdD, was born and raised in Poland, where she studied linguistics and world literature.

Eric J. López, PhD, is a professor at Texas A&M University–San Antonio (A&M-SA).

Thalia Marron is an elementary education major earning the bilingual endorsement from the Department of Curriculum and Instruction at Northern Illinois University.

Ruby Osoria is a Chicana doctoral student in education studies at the University of California, San Diego.

Brianna R. Ramirez is a Chicana doctoral candidate in education studies at the University of California, San Diego.

Dorota Silber-Furman, PhD, is a lecturer in the Department of Curriculum and Instruction at Tennessee Technological University (TTU).

Sunyung Song, PhD, is an assistant professor of education and English language learners at Athens State University.

Amy Van Buren, EdD, is a member of the faculty at the University of North Carolina at Pembroke.

Jancarlos Wagner-Romero, EdD, is an assistant professor of global and multicultural education at the University of Wisconsin–La Crosse. He previously served as an elected member of the New Orleans Public School Board, where he championed issues pertaining to Limited English Proficient communities and English language learners throughout the State of Louisiana.

Monica S. Yoo, PhD, is an associate professor and the secondary education program coordinator in the Department of Teaching and Learning at the University of Colorado, Colorado Springs.